Hiking Trails of NOVA SCOTIA

8th Edition

MICHAEL HAYNES

GOOSE LANE

Edited by Angela Williams.
Cover and interior design by Ryan Astle.
Printed in Canada by Transcontinental.
10 9 8 7 6 5 4 3 2

National Library of Canada Cataloguing in Publication Data

Haynes, Michael, 1955-
    Hiking trails of Nova Scotia

8th ed.
Includes bibliographical references and index.
ISBN 0-86492-291-4

1. Trails — Nova Scotia — Guidebooks.   2. Hiking — Nova Scotia — Guidebooks.
3. Nova Scotia — Guidebooks.   I. Title.

GV199.44.C2H54 2002   796.51'09716   C2002-900826-3

Published with the financial support of the Government of Canada through the Book Publishing Industry Development Program and the New Brunswick Culture and Sports Secretariat.

Goose Lane Editions
469 King Street
Fredericton, New Brunswick
CANADA E3B 1E5
www.gooselane.com

Contents

Introduction

Nova Scotia's character has always been defined by its intimate embrace with the Atlantic Ocean. Its 7000 km (4400 mi) of coastline is ragged with tiny bays and exposed headlands, endlessly pounded by the restless waves. Notwithstanding the narrow isthmus physically linking it to the mainland, Nova Scotia is an island, along with Newfoundland the easternmost outpost of North America, closer to Great Britain than to British Columbia. The harsh, rugged, and diverse landscape of the province is dominated by exposed bedrock, inadequately covered by infertile soils, and deeply etched by glaciers. And wherever you travel, you are never more than 60 km (40 mi) from the restless ocean and its demanding, incessant rhythm.

Hiking Trails of Nova Scotia, 8th Edition contains details of more than 60 trails and 750 km (475 mi) of walking and is, I hope, a worthwhile successor to the well-received 7th edition, published in 1995. Many of the trails are located in provincial and national parks; these tend to be of the highest quality, well maintained and signed, with special maps and background information. Most of the new trails profiled have been developed by community trail associations, and these are also developed to very high standards. In addition, many are shared-use, accommodating more recreational uses than just walking. However, a few of the hikes presented in this book are still unimproved: coastal walks following game trails and deserted roads leading to forgotten villages. Unlike the park trails, few of these possess signage or services of any kind. Whatever the hike may be, I hope you enjoy it.

NEW TRAILS

Owners of the 7th edition will notice that almost 75% of the listings in this edition are different, and that many good treks have disappeared. One reason for this is that many new trails have been built in the past seven years, so it is possible to profile many entirely new hikes. But do not throw out your old book! On page 250, you will find a section titled "Update of 7th Edition," which lists the trails dropped from the 8th edition and provides a brief indication of their condition.

Another reason is that, instead of one book, there is now a series of three books outlining hiking in Nova Scotia. In 1999, *Hiking Trails of Cape Breton* was published, listing 56 walks in that special part of the province. In 2000, *Trails of Halifax Regional Municipality* was released, a small volume profiling 30 walking paths near the Halifax-Dartmouth metropolitan area. With the release of the 8th edition of *Hiking Trails of Nova Scotia*, enthusiasts will have three books providing detailed information on more than 140 different hiking opportunities. Owners of the 7th edition will have 20 others that may still be used but are not found in one of the newer books. Never have there been so many options available for outdoor enthusiasts.

NEW FEATURES

Hiking Trails of Nova Scotia, 8th Edition includes two important innovations to conventional hiking guides first introduced in *Hiking Trails of Cape Breton*. Each trail description includes the Global Positioning System (GPS) co-ordinates for the principal trail access point, the *Start/parking*, as it is labelled on the accompanying map. Including this data will provide a safety bearing for anyone with a GPS unit. The GPS co-ordinates will also ease finding the start of unmarked trails and woods roads for the many users of this rapidly improving, convenient, and affordable technology.

The second important feature is a Cellphone Reception section with each trail description. Cellular telephones are often carried by hikers as a safety device. Unfortunately, people often do not confirm reception details before starting their treks, and coverage is not always available, particularly in some of the more remote or geologically difficult areas. By including this information, I hope to prevent hikers from discovering that their phones do not work at a critical time.

TRANS CANADA TRAIL

Since 1992, the concept of developing a multiuse recreational corridor stretching across the country has gradually been transformed from a dream to near reality. When completed, the Trans Canada Trail will be the longest recreational pathway in the world, exceeding 17,000 km (10,500 mi), and one of the largest volunteer projects ever achieved. In Nova Scotia, the Trans Canada Trail will extend from North Sydney, where the ferry from Newfoundland docks, to Amherst, the land connection with New Brunswick, and a spur will connect Halifax with the rest of Canada.

The TCT has been the focus of new trail development in the province, and many of the paths profiled in this book will be part of that system. In Cape Breton, the Old Branch Road, Lewis Mountain, and Mabou – Inverness are all on the main route of the TCT. In the Halifax Metro –

Marine Drive area, the Guysborough Nature Trail makes up part of the system. On the Sunrise Scenic Travelway, the Wallace Bridge, Jitney / Samson – Albion, and Tatamagouche – Denmark trails all belong to the TCT, as does the Cobequid Trail in the Glooscap region. Future extensions of the Trans Canada Trail in Nova Scotia may include the BLT Trail in the Halifax Metro – Marine Drive area, as well as the Aspotogan, Centennial, and Shelburne trails on the Lighthouse Route.

I hope you enjoy *Hiking Trails of Nova Scotia* and that the information in it helps you to better enjoy Nova Scotia's natural wonders.

HOW TO USE THIS BOOK

Hiking Trails of Nova Scotia is not a listing of all the trails in the province. In a recent survey, more than 500 different routes were identified as being used for hiking, although fewer than 200 were officially recognized as trails. What I have attempted to do is provide a detailed profile of 60 paths spread through every part of Nova Scotia, trying to include as many of the best experiences as possible.

For ease of use, I have grouped trails into roughly the same major regions used by the provincial department of tourism. The Evangeline, Glooscap, Lighthouse, and Sunrise

areas are identical to the regions found in the *Nova Scotia Scenic Travelways Map*. I combined the Halifax – Dartmouth area, which is mostly urban, with Marine Drive. Cape Breton Island is treated as one area.

I chose to balance the number of selections in each part of the province and to ensure that each region contained variety: some coastal trails, some inland, a few easy, and some more challenging. This occasionally meant that I left out very good trails because I had selected other, similar hikes in the same region. Kejimkujik National Park is an example: I selected only a few trails from a large number of possibilities. Whereas *Hiking Trails of Cape Breton* contains more than 50 routes, this volume includes only five Cape Breton trails, none of which were profiled in the Cape Breton book. The selection of the trails in *Hiking Trails of Nova Scotia,* 8th Edition is mine alone. If I have left out your favourite trail, please let me know.

Every regional section begins with a brief introduction, including a map indicating the approximate starting points of the trails. Each trail is a separate essay, incorporating an adaption of the most recent topographical map of the area, scaled to fit the book's pages, with the trail route superimposed upon it.

Every trail is described using the same basic format:

Name of Trail: gives the trail's official name if it is a maintained pathway.

Length: gives return-trip distance in kilometres and miles, rounded to the nearest half kilometre (quarter mile).

Hiking Time: a measurement based on an average walker's rate of 4 km (2.5 mi) per hour. This may not accurately reflect the time that you will require to complete any particular hike. Each person sets his or her own pace, which will vary according to weather conditions, length of the trail, and fitness level.

Type of Trail: indicates the footing that will be encountered.

Uses: mentions possible types of recreational use, including hiking, biking, cross-country skiing, horseback riding, snowmobiling, and ATV riding.

Facilities: indicates services, such as washrooms or water, that will be found along the trail.

Gov't Topo Map: identifies the National Topographic System 1:50 000 scale map showing the terrain covered by the trail.

Rating: expresses the difficulty of the trail on a scale from 1 to 5. Level 1 indicates that the trail is suitable for all fitness and experience levels; I recommend trails rated 5 for experienced and very fit outdoor people only. These ratings are based on considerations including length, elevation change, condition of treadway, and signage. Novices should choose level 1 and 2 hikes initially, and work up with experience. Starting at level 4 or 5 will only ensure that your hiking career includes punishment from the very beginning. Level 4 and 5 hikes include a brief indication of the characteristics that give them their higher rating.

Trailhead GPS Reference: indicates the latitude and longitude of the start/finish of the hike. This data was collected using a GARMIN GPS 12 XL Receiver. It is accurate to within 100 – 200 m/yd.

Each trail outline is divided into the following sections:

Access Information: explains how to get to the starting point of the trail from a community easily found on the basic Nova Scotia Tourism road map.

Introduction: gives background about the trail, including historical, natural, and geographical information, as well as my personal observations or recommendations.

Trail Description: provides a walkthrough of the hike, relating what I found when I last travelled this route. In every case, I describe junctions and landmarks from the perspective of someone following the trail in the direction that I have indicated. If travelling in the opposite direction, remember to reverse my bearings.

Cautionary Notes: warns of hunting season, cliffs, high winds, raging seas, or anything I believe you should be cautious about. Please take these warnings seriously. An accident in the wilderness is more dangerous than one in the city simply because of the remoteness from rapid assistance.

Cellphone Coverage: explains how well a cellular phone will work on this trail, including locations of dead spots. The data was collected using a Motorola StarTAC 6000e phone supplied by Aliant Mobility. If this particular phone was able to send and receive calls, other mobile telephone should do at least as well. New cellphone tower construction planned for the next several years should mean better coverage in the future for many of these trails.

Future Plans: mentions what, if anything, is intended in the way of changes to the trail or nearby area in the next few years.

Further Information: brochures are available for many of the trails, par-

ticularly those in parks. If so, I will mention it here, and I will also include specific relevant web sites.

The Trails at a Glance Chart, found on page 18, lists all of the trails, shows their length and degree of difficulty, indicates whether they are maintained, if there are facilities available, and provides an estimated length that will be required to complete the walk profiled.

EQUIPMENT

The recreation industry produces excellent equipment for outdoor enthusiasts, with the selection growing every year. I cannot provide recommendations about specific brands; each person must discover what works best for him or her. However, there are a few items that should always be carried whenever you enter the forest, even if only for a short hike. Doing so may help ensure that every hiking experience is an enjoyable and safe one.

By law, you must carry matches, a knife, and a compass when you travel in the woods in Nova Scotia. You are also required to know how to use the compass, something surprisingly few people can actually do, although most recreation departments offer courses in map and compass reading. Proper footwear is essential, and care should be taken selecting what you will use when hiking. There are also other

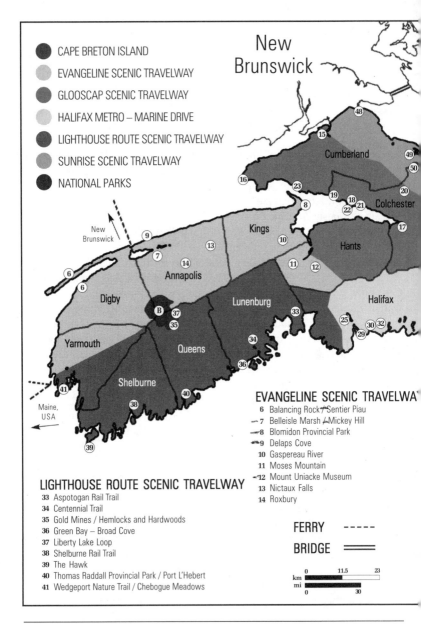

Legend

- CAPE BRETON ISLAND
- EVANGELINE SCENIC TRAVELWAY
- GLOOSCAP SCENIC TRAVELWAY
- HALIFAX METRO – MARINE DRIVE
- LIGHTHOUSE ROUTE SCENIC TRAVELWAY
- SUNRISE SCENIC TRAVELWAY
- NATIONAL PARKS

New Brunswick

Cumberland

New Brunswick

Kings

Colchester

Annapolis

Hants

Digby

Lunenburg

Halifax

Yarmouth

Queens

Maine, USA

Shelburne

EVANGELINE SCENIC TRAVELWAY

6 Balancing Rock / Sentier Piau
7 Belleisle Marsh / Mickey Hill
8 Blomidon Provincial Park
9 Delaps Cove
10 Gaspereau River
11 Moses Mountain
12 Mount Uniacke Museum
13 Nictaux Falls
14 Roxbury

LIGHTHOUSE ROUTE SCENIC TRAVELWAY

33 Aspotogan Rail Trail
34 Centennial Trail
35 Gold Mines / Hemlocks and Hardwoods
36 Green Bay – Broad Cove
37 Liberty Lake Loop
38 Shelburne Rail Trail
39 The Hawk
40 Thomas Raddall Provincial Park / Port L'Hebert
41 Wedgeport Nature Trail / Chebogue Meadows

FERRY -----

BRIDGE =====

km 0   11.5   23
mi 0   30

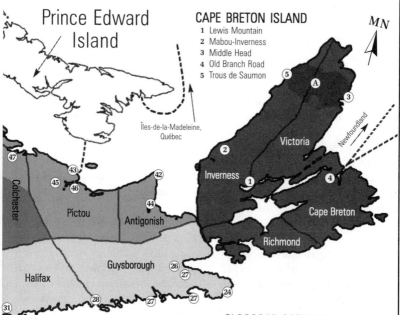

CAPE BRETON ISLAND

1 Lewis Mountain
2 Mabou-Inverness
3 Middle Head
4 Old Branch Road
5 Trous de Saumon

HALIFAX METRO – MARINE DRIVE

24 Black Duck Cove / Chapel Gully
25 BLT Trail
26 Guysborough Nature Trail
27 Guysborough Short Trails
28 Liscomb River
29 McNabs Island
30 Salmon River
31 Taylor Head Provincial Park
32 White Lake Wilderness Trail

NATIONAL PARKS

A Cape Breton Highlands National Park
B Kejimkujik National Park

GLOOSCAP SCENIC TRAVELWAY

15 Amherst Point Migratory Bird Sanctuary
16 Cape Chignecto Provincial Park
17 Cobequid Trail
18 Devil's Bend
19 Five Islands Provincial Park
20 High Head
21 Kenomee Canyon
22 Thomas Cove
23 Ward Falls / Partridge Island

SUNRISE SCENIC TRAVELWAY

42 Cape George
43 Caribou – Munroes Island Provincial Park
44 Fairmont Ridge
45 Fitzpatrick Mountain
46 Jitney / Samson – Albion Trails
47 Tatamagouche – Denmark
48 Tidnish Trail
49 Wallace Bay National Wildlife Area
50 Wallace Bridge

items that I believe you should always include as minimum equipment, even in summer.

Map: I always carry a map when I go hiking. Is it swampy? Are there cliffs? Are houses nearby? If I get lost, what direction do I follow to find people? In provincial and federal parks a special map of the trail is often available. Otherwise, I purchase the National Topographic System of Canada 1: 50 000 scale map of the area. With a map, I can get a sense of the terrain that I will be hiking.

Water: Nothing is more important than water. You can survive up to two weeks without food; you may die in as few as three days without water. I carry one litre per person on a hike of up to 10 km (6 mi), more if the distance is greater, if the day is particularly hot or humid, or if I am taking children with me. Dehydration occurs rapidly while hiking, and the accompanying headache or dizziness diminishes the pleasure of the experience. Drink small sips of water often and do not wait until you are thirsty to do so. Portable water filtration systems are available in any outdoor store, and are worth carrying, especially on hot summer treks.

Food: Though not really necessary on a day hike, I always carry something to snack on while I walk. Apples, trail mix, bagels: anything like this is good. Chocolate bars, chips, and other junk food are not the best choice for several reasons, but something is better than nothing.

Whistle: If you get lost and want to attract attention, a whistle will be heard far better than your voice, and is less likely to wear out from continuous use. Take one outside the house and give a couple of blasts. See how much attention you attract. (Blame me.)

First Aid Kit: When in the woods, even little problems become very important. A small first aid kit with bandages, gauze, tape, moleskin, etc., permits you to deal with blisters and bruises that require attention.

Garbage Bag: You should always carry your trash out: food wrappers, juice bottles, and even apple cores should go into the bag. If you are hiking on a well-used trail, you will probably find litter left behind by others. Take a moment to put as much as you can into your own garbage bag. If you don't do it, it probably won't get done.

Warm Sweater and/or Rain Jacket: Coastal weather is highly changeable, and Nova Scotia's weather is difficult to forecast accurately. Cold rains and high winds often combine for uncomfortable, possibly life-threatening, conditions. No matter how good the weather seems to be, always carry some protective clothing, particularly in spring and fall.

Backpack: You need something to carry everything, so I recommend that you invest in a quality daypack. It should have adjustable shoulder straps, a waist strap, a large inner pouch, and roomy outer pockets. The equipment listed earlier will fit easily inside a good pack and will sit comfortably on your back. After one or two trips, wearing it will become just another part of your walking routine. In fact, I never hike without my pack.

Optional (but Recommended) Equipment: sunscreen, hat, bug repellent, camera, binoculars, field guides, toilet paper, writing paper, and pen.

Really Optional Equipment: extra socks, tarp, rope, eating utensils, flashlight, towel, bathing suit, small stove, fuel, toothbrush, toothpaste, soap, and sleeping bag.

HAZARDS

Nova Scotia is home to few dangerous plants and animals. Four species of snake reside here, for example; all are harmless. Nevertheless, remember the following before you enter the woods.

Bears: Easily everyone's greatest fear while hiking, black bears live throughout the province, and I suggest obtaining Parks Canada's excellent brochure on them. Bears are rarely seen because they are generally afraid of people, perhaps partly because of the annual bear hunt throughout the province. They are primarily nocturnal and usually solitary, except during mating season and when a mother is caring for cubs. If you do happen to see bears, though, recognise that they are dangerous and unpredictable, and never, ever approach.

Bears are impressive and dangerous animals, growing to 215 kg (470 lb) and able to run up to 30 kph (19 mph). They are wild, unpredictable, and capable of causing you serious injury or even death, so behave accordingly. Making noise while you are walking will announce to a bear that you are nearby, and it will almost certainly withdraw before you see it. If a bear approaches, you should not try to run away or climb a tree. Black bears do both better and faster than people and will react to you as food attempting to escape. Instead, keep your face turned toward the bear while avoiding direct eye contact, and slowly back away from it. If the bear charges, scream, yell, and kick at it, which may frighten it away. You may drop your pack and hope it distracts the bear. If neither of these manoeuvres works, the best bet is to lie on the ground in a fetal position, with your arms drawn up to protect your face and neck, and attempt to remain still, however frightening and painful the experience might be. Most bears will be content to hit a person a few times, then withdraw.

The truth is, a bear might do almost anything, and sometimes they respond exactly the opposite to what you might expect. But before you decide never to hike again, please keep in mind that there has not been a recorded instance of a bear attacking a human being in Nova Scotia since the start of the twentieth century.

Cougars: Although rumoured to be present in Nova Scotia, none have been photographed, trapped, or shot in the past hundred years.

Poison Ivy: While relatively uncommon, it may be encountered on some coastal dunes and in a few other places. Managed trails will post warning signs. Intense itching is caused by an oil produced by the plant.

Ticks: Active in the Evangeline and Lighthouse regions from April to July, these small brown spider-like insects love to suck your blood! They do so by burrowing beneath the skin and hanging on until they are engorged. As ticks can carry some diseases dangerous to humans, you should notify your doctor if you find one that has fastened itself to you.

Lynx: Largely restricted to the Cape Breton Highlands, their principal diet is snowshoe hare. Lynx are very wary of humans.

Moose: These are extremely common in Cape Breton, especially in the Highlands. They are most likely to wander onto the road at dawn and dusk. Bulls weigh up to 550 kg (1200 lbs) and can knock a car off the highway. They can be unpredictable, especially during the fall rutting season. Moose are not just larger deer; treat them with as much respect and caution as you would a bear.

Hunting Season: Hunting is permitted in many of the areas covered in this book. Usually starting in early October, hunting season varies from year to year for different types of game. Contact the Department of Natural Resources for detailed information before going into the woods in the fall. No hunting is allowed on Sunday, but always wear a bright orange garment for safety. See www.gov.ns.ca/natr/hunt/ for details.

Weather: High winds along the coast are common, and the Cape Breton Highlands has the harshest environment in the Maritimes. Wind chill factor can become significant, even in late spring and early fall. (For example, you might start hiking inland at a temperature of +16°C (61°F). At the coastline, winds gust to 60 kph (37 mph). The wind chill equivalent becomes +6°C (43°F).) When wind chill combines with water chill from ocean spray, fog, or rain, hypothermia becomes probable. Carrying sweaters and rain gear is always a good idea.

Waugh River Bridge, Tatamagouche – Denmark Trail, Sunrise Scenic Travelway. MH

Trails at a Glance

Key	Difficulty Level: **1**= easy / **5**= difficult Facilities: **N**= none / **Y**= yes / **S**= seasonal Time: based on **4 km / hr** (d= day)

Trail Name	Difficulty Level					Length	Maintained Trail	Facilities	Time (hr)	Page
	1	2	3	4	5	Kilometers (miles)				
CAPE BRETON ISLAND										
Lewis Mountain			✓			9 km (5.5 mi)		N	2 – 3	22
Mabou-Inverness				✓		53 km (33 mi)	✓	Y	2 d	26
Middle Head	✓					4 km (2.5 mi)	✓	S	1 – 2	31
Old Branch Road		✓				16 km (10 mi)	✓	Y	4 – 5	35
Trous de Saumon			✓			13 km (8 mi)	✓	Y	4 – 5	39
EVANGELINE SCENIC TRAVELWAY										
Balancing Rock / Sentier Piau	✓					2.5 km (1.5 mi) 4.5 km (2.75 mi)	✓	Y	1	45
Belleisle Marsh / Mickey Hill	✓					3.5 km (2.25 mi) 2 km (1.25 mi)	✓	Y	1	49
Blomidon Provincial Park			✓			13 km (8 mi)	✓	S	4 – 5	53
Delaps Cove		✓				9.5 km (6 mi)	✓	Y	2 – 3	57
Gaspereau River		✓				9 km (5.5 mi)		N	2 – 3	60
Moses Mountain			✓			7.5 km (4.75 mi)		N	2 – 3	63
Mount Uniacke Museum			✓			12 km (7.5 mi)	✓	Y	4 – 5	68
Nictaux Falls				✓		20 km (12.5 mi)		N	4 – 6	72
Roxbury					✓	18 km (11.25 mi)		N	2 – 3	76

Trail Name	Difficulty Level					Length	Maintained Trail	Facilities	Time (hr)	Page
	1	2	3	4	5	Kilometers (miles)				
GLOOSCAP SCENIC TRAVELWAY										
Amherst Point Migratory Bird Sanctuary	✓					6 km (3.75 mi)	✓	N	1 – 2	83
Cape Chignecto Provincial Park				✓		52 km (32.5 mi)	✓	S	3 d	87
Cobequid Trail		✓				13 km (8 mi)	✓	Y	3 – 4	93
Devil's Bend				✓		13 km (8 mi)	✓	Y	4 – 5	96
Five Islands Provincial Park			✓			11 km (7 mi)	✓	S	3 – 4	100
High Head			✓			9 km (5.5 mi)	✓	S	2 – 4	105
Kenomee Canyon				✓		21 km (13 mi)	✓	Y	6 – 11	108
Thomas Cove	✓					7 km (4.5 mi)	✓	Y	2 – 3	113
Ward Falls / Partridge Island		✓				7 km (4.5 mi) 3.25 km (2 mi)	✓	Y	2 – 3 1	117
HALIFAX METRO – MARINE DRIVE										
Black Duck Cove / Chapel Gully	✓					3.5 km (2 mi) 4.5 km (2.75 mi)	✓	Y	1 – 2	125
BLT Trail			✓			19 km (12 mi)	✓	N	5 – 6	129
Guysborough Nature Trail				✓		33 km (21 mi)	✓	Y	9 – 12	133
Guysborough Short Trails (Lundys Firetower, Port Bickerton, and Tor Bay)	✓					4 km (2.5 mi) 3.5 km (2.25 mi) 1.5 km (1 mi)	✓	S	1 – 2	138
Liscomb River			✓			9.5 km (6 mi)	✓	S	3 – 4	144
McNabs Island		✓				7 km (4.5 mi)		Y	2 – 3	148
Salmon River				✓		12 km (7.5 mi)		N	4 – 5	152
Taylor Head Provincial Park				✓		18 km (11.25 mi)	✓	S	6 – 7	156
White Lake Wilderness Trail					✓	17 km (10.5 mi)	✓	Y	7 – 9	160

Trail Name	Difficulty Level					Length	Maintained Trail	Facilities	Time (hr)	Page
	1	2	3	4	5	Kilometers (miles)				
LIGHTHOUSE ROUTE SCENIC TRAVELWAY										
Aspotogan Rail Trail				✓		23 km (14.5 mi)	✓	Y	5 – 7	167
Centennial Trail		✓				16 km (10 mi)	✓	Y	3 – 5	170
Gold Mines / Hemlocks and Hardwoods	✓					3 km (2 mi) 6 km (4 mi)	✓	Y	1 – 2	174
Green Bay – Broad Cove			✓			12 km (7.5 mi)		N	3 – 4	180
Liberty Lake Loop					✓	60 km (37.5 mi)	✓	Y	3 d	183
Shelburne Rail Trail				✓		22 km (13.5 mi)	✓	Y	4 – 7	189
The Hawk		✓				8.5 km (5.25 mi)		Y	2 – 3	193
Thomas Raddall Provincial Park / Port L'Hebert		✓				7 km (4.5 mi) 3 km (2 mi)	✓	S/Y	1 – 2	197
Wedgeport Nature Trail / Chebogue Meadows	✓					5.4 km (3.5 mi) 5.5 km (3.5 mi)	✓	S	1 – 2	202
SUNRISE SCENIC TRAVELWAY										
Cape George				✓		12 km (7.5 mi)	✓	Y	4 – 6	209
Caribou – Munroes Island Provincial Park		✓				11.5 km (7.25 mi)	✓	S	2 – 3	213
Fairmont Ridge			✓			11 km (7 mi)	✓	Y	3 – 4	217
Fitzpatrick Mountain				✓		16 km (10 mi)	✓	N	4 – 6	221
Jitney / Samson – Albion Trails	✓					3 km (2 mi) 7 km (4.5 mi)	✓	Y	1 – 2	225
Tatamagouche – Denmark				✓		21 km (13 mi)	✓	Y	6 – 8	230
Tidnish Trail		✓				8 km (5 mi)	✓	S	2 – 3	234
Wallace Bay National Wildlife Area	✓					4 km (2.5 mi)	✓	N	1 – 2	238
Wallace Bridge		✓				8 km (5 mi)	✓	S	2	241

Glendyer Brook, Mabou – Inverness Trail. MH

Lewis Mountain

Length: 9 km (5.5 mi) rtn
Hiking Time: 2-3 hr
Type of Trail: old woods road
Uses: hiking, biking, horseback
   riding, snowmobiling, ATV
   riding, cross-country skiing
Facilities: none
Gov't Topo Map: Lake Ainslie 11
   K/3 and Whycocomagh 11 F/14
Rating (1-5): 3
Trailhead GPS Reference:
   N 45° 59' 33.1" W 61° 00'29.0"

Access Information: From Whyco-comagh, drive northeast on Highway 105 toward Sydney for 11 km (7 mi) to Exit 6. At the intersection, turn left onto a dirt track next to the electrical transformer. Park behind the transformer. The trail begins at the far end of what appears to be a small gravel pit. The path entrance is difficult to see.

Introduction: Climbing from near Whycocomagh Bay to the heights of the Cape Breton Highlands Plateau, more than 700 m (2300 ft) above, the Lewis Mountain Road is a hiker's delight. The first half of the trail must be one of the prettiest walks in this book, following an always-lively brook up a narrow ravine through a lush hardwood forest alive with birds. Although it is a former road crossing

the Highlands between the Bras D'Or Lakes and Lake Ainslie, it is as if the route was designed for hiking, wide enough for two to walk side-by-side yet narrow enough to provide enclosed and comfortable snugness.

Families will enjoy this walk, although the constant climb may prevent some from continuing to its end. For many, turning back when path and brook diverge will provide the best scenic experience. Energetic hikers will want to follow the path to the junction where I have ended my description, and mountain bikers may wish to continue the rest of the distance, about another 5 km (3 mi) to Lake Ainslie.

Trail Description: The path starts uphill immediately, clearly an old road. However, the treadway is grass-covered, and very pleasant walking. The trees near the start include many hardwoods, providing overhead cover and shade, and the slope of the steep hillsides may be visible through their leaves. Three large power lines cross overhead 250 m/yd from the start and the wide cut enables you to view along the base of the highlands. MacPhersons Brook cannot yet be seen, but you will probably hear it bubbling away to the left.

On the far side of the power lines cut, the trail curves gently left and into

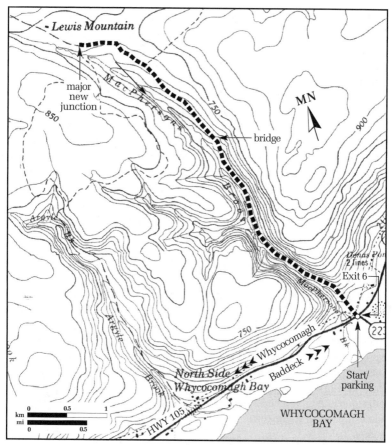

Lewis Mountain

the narrow gorge carved by MacPhersons Brook. You are entering the most beautiful portion of the walk, with steep slopes both above and below the path, and on both sides of the narrow brook. In the protected microclimate of the ravine, hardwoods cling to the hillsides, which are themselves crowned with dense thickets of spruce and balsam fir. In summer, the beech and maples provide shade, in fall, an anarchy of colour, in spring and winter, unobstructed views of the rapidly ascending path.

About 750 m/yd from the start, watch for a rock face on the right. To its left is a wonderful, large swimming hole. Just below the pool is a particularly vigorous cascade, almost a small waterfall. Above the pool, the stream is a series of small cascades, churning over the mossy rocks lining its banks, offering numerous places to dip your feet in the refreshing mountain water. The short distance between the path and the brook, however, is often steep and covered with small, loose rocks hidden by fallen leaves, so tread carefully.

The climb is never very steep, although it is consistent. It is rendered easier because of the excellence of the treadway, which has a solid surface and is well-drained. At 900 m/yd, the trail nearly levels, and, by 1 km (.6 mi), path and brook are side-by-side. Bare rock on the right-hand slope is frequent, and a few wet areas begin to appear in the former road surface where small streams cross the trail. At 1.5 km (1 mi), you may notice an old stone foundation on the left, and there are even some rusted metal scraps inside.

By 2 km (1.5 mi), the path has climbed far away from MacPhersons Brook, and the hillside is much less steep. About 200 m/yd further on you reach the remains of a small bridge, barely more than a large culvert, in an almost open area. Most walkers may prefer to turn around at this point, as the most scenic portion of the walk is over. MacPhersons Brook will rarely be seen any more, although it will still be heard in the quiet gully.

At 2.5 km (2 mi), the path soon becomes much rougher, almost a stream bed, sunken much lower than the ground on either side. The soil in the treadway has been eroded away, often the footing is a jumble of small rocks. At 3 km (2 mi), the old road contours into a narrow gully, which is crossed by an intact wooden bridge, by far the largest structure you will encounter. Several more of these little gullies require the path to curve around them.

Shortly after crossing the bridge, you will notice that the forest has changed to almost completely softwood and that there appear to be an unusual number of dead trees. These are the remains of the vast Cape Breton forests of white spruce killed by a massive infestation of spruce budworm in the 1970s. Most of the trees on the highland plateau were devastated, and the effects are still visible. These low, open woods make excellent habitat for moose, however, so do not be surprised if you will need to dance around frequent earthy reminders of their presence on the path.

The remainder of the walk is quite rough, though nearly level, and sometimes with thick vegetation growing onto the trail. At 4.1 km (2.5 mi) there is a distinct junction but keep left. Less than 500 m/yd later, 4.5 km (2.75 mi) from the start, the Lewis Mountain

Road reaches a major junction with a very wide logging road. To the right is the route of the Trans Canada Trail; the left route will descend the plateau to the shores of Lake Ainslie. Turn around and retrace your route to the start.

Cautionary Notes: Hunting is permitted in this area. Seasons will vary according to species, but generally wear hunter orange from early October through to early December. Hunting is prohibited on Sundays, but caution is still recommended.

Cellphone Reception: Coverage is rarely adequate to complete a call beyond the power lines, either in the ravine or on the plateau.

Future Plans: Lewis Mountain will soon be developed as part of the Trans Canada Trail System.

Mabou – Inverness

Length: 53 km (33 mi) rtn
Hiking Time: 2 days
Type of Trail: abandoned rail line
Uses: hiking, biking, horseback
  riding, snowmobiling, ATV
  riding, cross-country skiing
Facilities: none
Gov't Topo Map:
  Lake Ainslie 11 K/3
Rating (1-5): 5 [distance]
Trailhead GPS Reference:
  N 46° 04' 26.4" W 61° 21' 25.6"

Access Information: From Port Hastings, drive 60 km (37.5 mi) north on Highway 19. The trailhead is located in Mabou, just before the bridge crossing the river, where the railway intersects the highway. There is parking space available on both sides of the road, or you can begin from the parking lot of the nearby Hostel.

Introduction: This is one of the most attractive inland sections of abandoned rail line in Nova Scotia. The view of the Mabou Highlands from the Mabou River is stunning, and the stretch alongside the river to Glendyer Station is a paradise for birders. Although I have profiled this as one long hike, you can start at Mabou Station and turn around at Glendyer Station, 9 km (5.5 mi) return. This walk is suitable for anybody who is comfortable with the distance.

Trail Description: Your route must cross the highway, and you do so near the entrance to the hostel and before the road bridges the Mabou River. The trail enters a dense section of hardwood for the next 500 m/yd; the village of Mabou is visible through the leaves on your left. When

The Coal and Rail Museum, Inverness, the end of the trail. MH

you emerge from the trees, between the river and a small pond draining MacNeils Brook, the view of Mabou , its white church steeple rising out of the trees, is magnificent. You cross another railway trestle bridge here, and one more a few hundred metres/yards further on at Rankins Brook.

The trail now closely borders the broad and meandering Mabou River with marshy areas perfect for ducks on both sides of the rail line. Study the high dead trees out in the marshy areas. If you do not see at least one bald eagle, you have not looked closely enough. For the next 3.5 km (2.25 mi), your attention will probably be entirely focused on the river, and the broad marshy grasslands of its floodplain.

When you reach a steel truss bridge, you are nearly at Glendyer Station. Continue another 250 m/yd, and you encounter a second of these large structures. Both have been recently decked by the Canadian Army Engineers. After a further 100 m/yd, you cross paved Highway 252, and the path now parallels a dirt road. About 500 m/yd along, road and trail briefly share the same route beneath a rocky slope. A beautiful brook is crossed on a small steel bridge 2 km (1.25 mi) from Highway 252.

Past this point, the trail moves away from the road, staying close to Glendyer Brook, curving right in a broad gradual arc before settling down onto a relatively straight route. The trail is shrouded by forest and is lower than the ground on either side, for a considerable distance. ATV trails and old woods roads connect, but, except for a small bridge at 10 km (6 mi) and another at Glendyer Brook, where it is often quite wet, there are few features. The chance of seeing wildlife is excellent; when I passed through, I saw a bobcat twice.

For the next 2 km (1.25 mi), the treadway is often wet. You are entering the Black River valley, a low swampy area of thick, peaty soil bordering Lake Ainslie. When the woods begin to give way to fields, you have almost reached the Blackstone Road, 12 km (7.5 mi) from Mabou Station. The view is striking. To your left, the Mabou Highlands dominate the skyline; directly ahead, but in the distance, the low ridge of the Cape Breton Highlands is visible. On the right, a large farm complex sits atop a small cleared hill. The route follows Black River with frequent marshes and beaver-created pools lapping at the edges of the treadway. Not at the first bridge, 3.5 km (2.25 mi) from Blackstone Road, but at the second, a longer trestle over Black River 900 m/yd later, you will gain cellphone reception for the first time in the surrounding open meadows.

You cross paved West Lake Ainslie Road after 17 km (11 mi) of trekking. Trail and road remain very close,

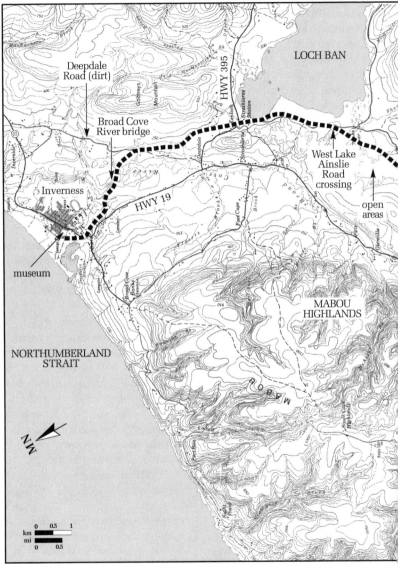

Deepdale
Road (dirt)

Broad Cove
River bridge

Inverness

museum

HWY 19

HWY 395

LOCH BAN

West Lake
Ainslie
Road
crossing

open
areas

MABOU
HIGHLANDS

NORTHUMBERLAND
STRAIT

NW

km   0   0.5   1
mi   0   0.5

Mabou – Inverness (Part 1)

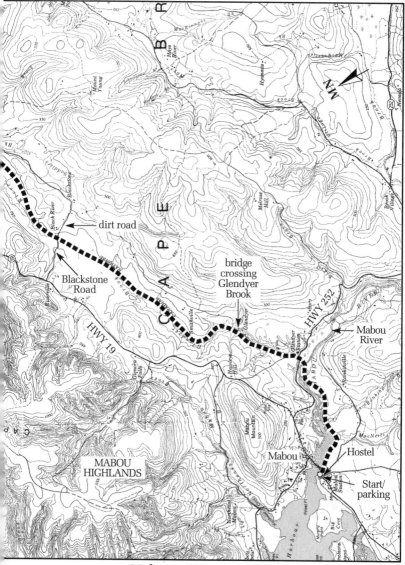

Mabou – Inverness (Part 2)

and, on your right, Loch Ban is visible through the trees. Two kilometres (1.25 mi) later, the trail comes to the shore of the lake, providing possibly the best view on the hike. You have only 700 m/yd, however, before you reach Strathlorne Station and the route turns away from the water.

The trail crosses Highway 395 at the road junction next to the Kenloch Presbyterian Church, 20 km (12.5 mi) into the hike. On the other side of the road, houses and fields are visible to the right on the open slopes of Godfreys Mountain. Re-entering a section of thick, young trees, you will see little until you cross the Deepdale dirt road at 23 km (14.5 mi). One kilometre (.6 mi) later you reach the marvellous trestle bridge crossing high above Broad Cove River. Since almost all of your walk has been overshadowed by hills, this sudden exposed walk, 25 m/yd above a little valley, is somewhat of a shock. For the final km (.6 mi), you will have views of the Mabou Highlands on the left, and soon buildings come into view. You will cross busy Highway 19 after a trek of 26 km (16.25 mi), and are now surrounded by the houses of Inverness. Continue another 500 m/yd, and finish the walk at the Inverness Coal and Railway Museum.

I recommend spending the night in Inverness and returning the next day along the same route.

Cautionary Notes: You must cross several roads, including Highway 19 in Inverness. These roads can be busy, and local drivers are still not accustomed to trail users.

Hunting is permitted in woods near the trail. Wear hunter orange in the fall.

Cellphone Coverage: There is no coverage except from Lake Ainslie to Inverness.

Future Plans: The entire abandoned rail line from Port Hastings to Inverness has been designated as a future route of the Trans Canada Trail. Expect substantial improvements to signage and access points over the next few years.

Middle Head

Length: 4 km (2.5 mi) rtn
Hiking Time: 1-2 hr
Type of Trail: former road, walking path
Uses: hiking, cross-country skiing
Facilities: garbage cans, benches
Gov't Topo Map: Ingonish 11 K/9
Rating (1-5): 1
Trailhead GPS Reference:
    N 46° 39' 19.5" W 60° 22' 19.9"

Access Information: Less than a kilometre from the park entrance at Ingonish, signs clearly indicate the trailhead. Turning off the Cabot Trail onto the road to Keltic Lodge, drive 2 km (1.25 mi) to the main resort building and park behind. Should you encounter a gate closing the road, found sometimes in the off-season, you must walk an additional kilometre (.6 mi) (each way).

Introduction: Dividing Ingonish Bay almost equally, Middle Head, a narrow rocky finger extending into the ocean and flanked by magnificent sandy beaches, is one of the most recognizable sights in Nova Scotia. Home of the renowned Keltic Lodge resort, it is known as "Geganisg," or "remarkable place" to the Mi'kmaq. Middle Head was once a base for both Native and European fishers. Much of the trail was once the carriage road connecting a summer estate, where Keltic Lodge now stands, with the fishing village.

After 1 km (.6 mi), a branch loops

Black-Capped Chickadee

If you see tiny, energetic birds flitting among the trees, chances are you will soon hear the easily identifiable call: *chik-a-dee-dee*. Black-capped chickadees are found throughout the province, and are quite comfortable around people. They are curious as well, and a slow, steady *pish-pish-pish*, repeated while standing motionless, can soon result in several of the little birds landing in nearby trees to get a closer look. If you put seeds in your hand and sit very still, they may land momentarily on your fingertips.

A related species, the boreal chickadee, can be distinguished by its brownish-grey head. Both types of chickadee remain in Nova Scotia throughout the year, and, in winter, can often be seen in company with golden-crowned kinglets and red-breasted nuthatches hunting for insects on trees.

Roger Tory Peterson (PMNL, GNL)

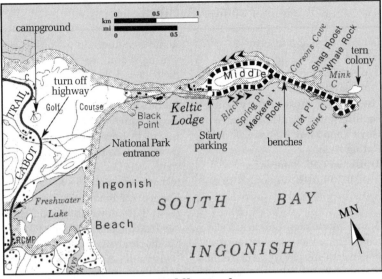

Middle Head

back to return to the opposite side of the point. I counsel this option for some, because a fairly steep hill is encountered in the second half of the walk. Fortunately, there are several benches along the route, permitting rest for the weary.

Experienced hikers may overlook Middle Head because of its shortness, but I recommend they reconsider. With the tern colony at the point, fishing settlement ruins, and dramatic views, this trail is well worth anyone's attention.

Trail Description: From the parking lot, climb the stairs and turn right. Numerous interpretive signs describe the history of the area. Pass between the concrete pillars, the remains of the estate's gate, and go by the drinking trough and benches. The track is wide and level until a short uphill is encountered just before reaching a junction. Turn left to return to Keltic Lodge, right to continue the full hike.

The trail descends fairly steeply, passing several benches, until it reaches a grassy field at a very narrow point of the peninsula. This was the location of the fishing village that was active until the early 1900s. Climbing the far side of the field, you might notice that almost no hardwoods remain. This far out on the point, salt spray kills almost every species of tree. Only white spruce, growing densely for protection and gnarled by wind into stunted stands called krummholz, can live here.

The trail remains sheltered by trees for most of this last kilometre, although views of Cape Smokey and Ingonish Beach are frequent. Instead of grass, footing becomes a carpet of roots and spruce needles, and, nearing the headland, the path narrows. Overlooking Seine Cove is another bench and interpretive panel. An unmarked junction permits the option of a short jaunt left to the north side of the point and an observation site viewing Mink Cove. Continue to the right to reach the headland, only 200 m/yd away.

You emerge suddenly from the shelter of the trees onto the exposed and barren point. This grassy area is criss-crossed with paths made by decades of tourists. To the south are several foundations of abandoned fishing shelters and a splendid view of Cape Smokey. To the north, Ingonish Island is the prominent landmark. Tiny Steering Island, just offshore, is covered in ropes to protect tern chicks from voracious predatory gulls. Guillemots, cormorants, and several species of gull are frequently sighted from this location. Expect it to be much cooler here than at Keltic Lodge.

To return to the start, retrace your steps, at least as far as the junction at the top of the long hill. For a different route, turn right here and follow the track as it works its way around the north side of Middle Head. The views of North Bay and Ingonish are superb, and the broad, level trail makes marvellous walking. Note the old stone work and its excellent condition; several tree cuttings have been made to permit clear views, and benches have been placed to take advantage of them. After 750 m/yd, the path cuts back left, climbing higher ground to complete the loop. It rejoins the old carriage road closer to the resort than to your starting position, but in sight of the parking lot.

Cautionary Notes: The very tip of Middle Head is exposed to high winds and waves. Be careful near the water's edge. Be mindful of steep cliffs near the trail border at several places, particularly if children accompany you.

Steering Island at the tip of Middle Head is home to a colony of common and arctic terns. At certain times of the year, this end of the trail will be closed for their protection.

Cellphone Reception: Adequate throughout.

Further Information: Parks Canada produces numerous brochures, including a hiking route pamphlet, and all trails are indicated on their special topographical map of the entire park. These can be obtained at park information centres or from Les Amis du Plein Air bookstore in Cheticamp.

Krummholz

The effects of high winds and salt spray can be seen in the trees that grow near the ocean, especially those at the edge of barrens. Few species, none hardwoods, can survive the massive amounts of salt that are deposited on them by the fogs that roll in from offshore. Almost all the trees found by the ocean edge are the very hardy white spruce.

Fierce Atlantic gales produce a most dramatic visual effect. They stunt and shape the white spruce, causing dense branching that grows in the opposite direction from the prevailing winds. Several trees will cluster together in thick stands, forming a dense curtain of branches that insulates the lee side and protects the walker on a blustery day.

Krummholz is a German word meaning "crooked wood."

Old Branch Road

Length: 16 km (10 mi) rtn
Hiking Time: 4-5 hr
Type of Trail: abandoned rail line
Uses: hiking, biking, horseback riding, snowmobiling, ATV riding, cross-country skiing, automobiles, logging vehicles
Facilities: picnic tables, benches, garbage cans, outhouses
Gov't Topo Map: Sydney 11 K/1
Rating (1-5): 2
Trailhead GPS Reference:
    N 44° 21' 49.5" W 65° 10' 58.4"

Access Information: From the direction of Sydney, drive along Highway 125, turning off at Exit 2. Turn left on Johnston Road and drive for 500 m/yd. There is a parking area on your left just past the Georges River road sign and the trail starts here.

Introduction: The Old Branch Road Trail, a project of the Cape Breton County Trails Association, became the first section of the Trans Canada Trail to officially be opened on Cape Breton Island. On July 3, 2001, the association held an official opening ceremony at the trailhead near North Sydney. More than 150 people were present to hear representatives from the community, the trail association, and local politicians talk about what the new trail means to the area.

I think bicyclists will enjoy this trail. The improved gravel surface is wonderful for them. Families will find this an easy walk because it is

Start of the Old Branch Road Trail, Georges River. MH

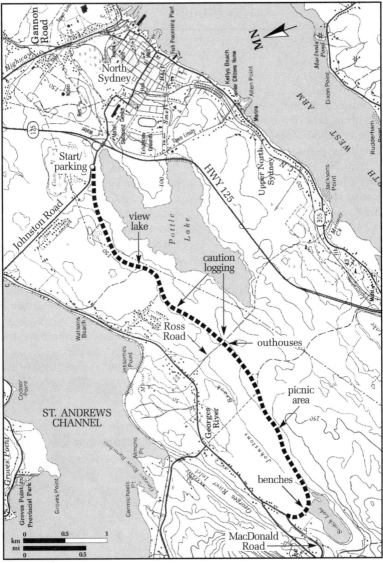

Old Branch Road

nearly level throughout. ATV riders frequently use the trail, as do loggers working nearby. This is one of the few officially maintained trails anywhere that is also still in use as a road, although only local landowners may drive their vehicles on it.

Trail Description: The Old Branch Road Trail begins beside Johnston Road as a very wide gravelled path – at least 5 m/yd broad. When you reach the trailhead information sign, about 250 m/yd from the trailhead, you will read that this is a shared-use trail that is open to some motorized vehicles, and that it has a 25 kph (16 mph) speed limit. A popular alternate starting point is the cemetery parking lot on the hill above the sign.

For the first kilometre (.6 mi), the treadway is freshly covered with gravel, and many vehicle entrances connect on either side of the path. However, as soon as you leave the trailhead sign, you will not see another residence, since the woods close in on both sides of the path. Between 1.5 and 2 km (1 mi), you will be able to view fields on either side of the route, and you also get a glimpse of Pottle Lake to the left.

There is quite a bit of evidence of activity in the woods along the path; at 3 km (2 mi), you should notice a trail sign saying, "Caution: Logging." The path has narrowed quite a bit at this point, and the trees on either side have grown up enough that you are shaded except near noon.

Watch for outhouses in the woods to the left slightly beyond the 4 km (2.5 mi) mark, just after a dirt road crosses the trail. There is also another trailhead information sign posted at this junction, Ross Road. If you follow this to the right, you will reach a paved road in 1 km (.6 mi). After Ross Road, you continue through thickly wooded terrain with no views for a further 1.6 km (1 mi) until a clear-cut provides some opening on the right. You will see a house more than 500 m/yd in the distance; the first habitation you will have seen since you started your walk.

At 6 km (4 mi), you will reach a newly built wooden bridge crossing a small creek. The association has made a picnic area here, with tables and benches. The trail narrows beyond this point, and the trees bordering it appear older and more attractive. After one more kilometre (.6 mi), you quite suddenly emerge into a clearing. Small Scotch Lake, hugged by high hills, is located on your left. Tiny Johnstons Brook flows from it near the trail.

As you approach Scotch Lake, the path very closely follows along the edge of the water. However, it also passes through a rail cut with quite high ridges on both sides of the pathway. This is a very pretty section of the route. Just on the far side of the cut, the association has placed a bench and signage at the edge of the lake. This tranquil spot will certainly entice you to stop and spend a few minutes just looking over the water.

From here, only a further 500 m/yd remain until you reach the end of the trail at gravelled MacDonald Road. Retrace your route to the trailhead at North Sydney.

Cautionary Notes: You may encounter logging vehicles, backhoes, trucks, and other motorized vehicles sharing the path. Move to the side of the trail and let them pass.

Hunting is permitted in adjacent woods. Wear hunter orange in the fall, from October on.

Cellphone Reception: Adequate throughout.

Future Plans: Old Branch Road will eventually become part of the Trans Canada Trail system.

Trous de Saumon

Length: 13 km (8 mi) rtn
Hiking Time: 4-5 hr
Type of Trail: former road, walking paths
Uses: hiking, mountain biking, cross-country skiing
Facilities: outhouses, campsite, firewood, showers, shelters, picnic tables, garbage cans, water
Gov't Topo Map:
Cheticamp River 11 K/10
Rating (1-5): 3
Trailhead GPS Reference:
N 46° 38' 48.8" W 60° 56' 59.4"

Trous de Saumon. MH

Access Information: Enter the Cape Breton Highlands National Park through the Cheticamp entrance, crossing over the Cheticamp River. The park visitor center, including Les Amis du Plein Air bookstore, is situated between the bridge and the entrance kiosk. Park your car in its lot, and continue on foot through the campground toward the group camping area. The road nearest the river is the trail, although the sign is difficult to see, being just a tiny marker perhaps 20 m/yd past the large "Department vehicles only beyond this point" notice. Do not follow the road heading sharply left up the hill.

Introduction: Cheticamp River is

known for its fishing; the name of this hike is French for "salmon pools," and anglers are often found at the deep lagoons beneath the several cataracts along the route. This path was developed to attract anglers to the park by providing easier access to the best spots. If you wish to try your luck, remember that you must use a tied fly and have a licence.

Novices can enjoy this hike. As far as the first pool and warden's cabin, the route is road width and well-graded, suitable for almost anyone. Beyond this point, however, the trail becomes progressively more difficult, more suitable for experienced, fit hikers.

Trail Description: A metal gate pre-

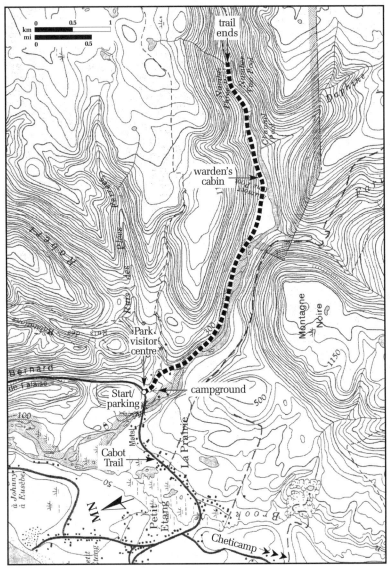

Trous de Saumon

vents vehicular access, and the path is broad and well-graded, wide enough for two. Initially climbing a small hill, the trail soon descends to near river level. At first the path stays near the northern slope. Ample evidence exists of the flooding that occurs during spring runoff in this narrow valley. There are several lovely hardwood glades of pin cherry and striped maple underneath, with larger maples, beech, and oak overhead. Benches are available for those who wish to sit and enjoy the shade.

In this first portion of the hike, massive Montagne Noire dominates the southern side of the valley. Do not be surprised if you hear the occasional sound of a motor, as a road from the community of La Prairie parallels the river on the other bank. After nearly 3 km (2 mi), you will notice the broad valley cut by Faribault Brook dividing the southern skyline. Soon the canyon walls of the Cheticamp River valley begin to constrict.

Shortly after you cross two bridges, you reach the first salmon pool. The path divides, with fishers heading to the water and hikers heading uphill. Signs remind anglers of proper fishing etiquette. An observation area permits the sharp-sighted, at the right time of year, to glimpse Atlantic salmon in the deep pool below. Just past this spot, on the left cresting a small hill, is a warden's cabin. Up to

this point, the hike can be completed by almost anyone, and returning to the start now constitutes a respectable 7 km (4.5 mi) amble.

Continuing on, both valley and trail narrow considerably. Whenever the river strays northward the trail is forced to climb up the steep slope; when the stream is near the south slope the path descends again. Channel Pool is only a few hundred metres/ yards beyond the cabin, and the second pool less than a kilometre (.6 mi) beyond that. Here is a small emergency shelter, and a sign stating that bicycles may proceed no further.

The trail now definitely becomes more challenging, climbing steeply to pass over the cataract above the second pool. It follows a narrow ravine deep into the hillside before crossing a brook on a plank bridge with a handrail. From the enveloping slopes, occasional falls of stone, known as talus, might make the walking uneven. The views of the steep-sided and V-shaped valley beyond, however, are magnificent.

All too quickly, it seems, the path opens up into a small clearing and abruptly ends at the third pool. With plenty of bare rock by the river's edge, it is a lovely spot to have a snack. Steep cliff walls impede further impromptu trekking. Unless you plan to fish, retrace your steps back to the parking lot and the information centre. Fortunately, you will find that most of the return trip is downhill, with the exception of the final climb before you reach the campground.

Cautionary Notes: During the spring melt the Cheticamp River runs very fast and often overflows its banks. Inquire about conditions before hiking in late March, April, and early May. Remember, weather conditions change very quickly in the highlands. Always carry some warm clothing, even in summer.

Cellphone Coverage: Reception is limited near the Park Administration Centre and the trailhead. No signal can be obtained upstream.

Further Information: Parks Canada produces several brochures, including a hiking route pamphlet, and this trail is indicated on their special topographical map of the park. These can be purchased at the information centres at Cheticamp and Ingonish.

Balancing Rock. MH

Anse des Leblanc, Sentier Piau. MH

Balancing Rock / Sentier Piau

Length: 2.5 km (1.5 mi) rtn
(Balancing Rock)
4.5 km (2.75 mi) rtn
(Sentier Piau)

Hiking Time: 1 hr

Type of Trail: gravelled treadway, boardwalk

Uses: hiking

Facilities: garbage cans, outhouses, benches, tables

Gov't Topo Map:
Church Point 21 B/8

Rating (1-5): 1

Trailhead GPS Reference:
N 44° 22' 03.3" W 66° 14' 07.6" (Balancing Rock)
N 44° 23' 16.2" W 66° 03' 44.4" (Sentier Piau)

Access Information:

Balancing Rock: From Digby, follow Highway 217 to East Ferry, almost 50 km (31.5 mi). Take the ferry to Tiverton, and continue on Highway 217 for 4 km (2.5 mi). Parking is on the left.

Sentier Piau: From Digby, follow Highway 101 for 33 km (20.5 mi) to Exit 28. Turn right, and follow Highway 1 about 4 km (2.5 mi) in the community of Belliveaus Cove. The trailhead is on the right just past the harbour. There is a road sign.

Introduction:

Balancing Rock: One of the most famous scenic destinations in the province, the Balancing Rock is a slender column of basalt perched in an apparently impossible position. Yet it has been this way, geologists maintain, for many thousands or even millions of years. Thousands of visitors endure the steep descent and climb each year to take pictures of this remarkable sight. Never expect to be alone on this trail.

Sentier Piau: Belliveaus Cove Trail was completed in late 1999, and is a walk for almost anybody. There are no hills, the treadway is well-defined and gravelled. It should be pleasant for families and seniors. Backcountry hikers will not enjoy it, but the scenery is pleasant and the interpretive panels are interesting.

Trail Description:

Balancing Rock: The first 900 m/yd is a fairly level, straight walk from the highway to the top of the cliff facing St. Marys Bay. The remaining 300 m/yd is an extensively developed system of stairs, platforms, and railings attempting to ease the passage down the steep hillside. The sign at the trailhead says there are

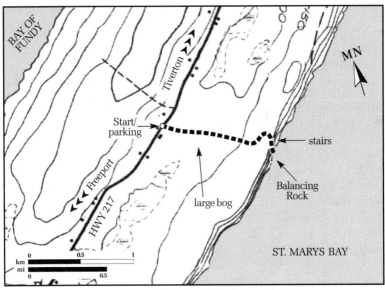

Balancing Rock

169 steps; you will notice them all on the return climb.

The path ends on a platform nearly at sea level facing the Balancing Rock. Across St. Marys Bay, the buildings of Church Point and the Acadian shore are easily visible. Interpretive panels on the platform explain the geological forces that produced this unique rock formation. When you have finished, climb the stairs and return the way you hiked in.

Sentier Piau: Sentier Piau, or Piau's Trail, starts at the mouth of the Isaacs Lake Brook at a large parking area beside the wharf where there are tables, an outhouse, benches, and an interpretive panel including a map. There is also a guest book and a donation box for trail maintenance. The trail takes its name from Pierre "Piau" Belliveau, who spent the winter of 1755 on the point with 120 refugees fleeing the deportation around Port Royal.

The path heads left along the thick, high cobble bordering Anse des Leblanc. Much of the route is visible, because Pointe à Major is low and almost completely empty of trees. The treadway is wide enough for two to walk side-by-side and surfaced with crusher dust. At low tide, Anse des Leblanc becomes a long, muddy beach extending several hundred

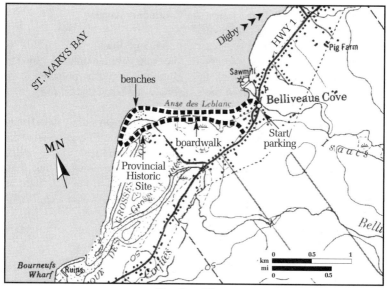

Sentier Piau

metres from the high water mark. The sand is covered with numerous species of birds feasting on the marine life exposed. Expect to see a few people digging clams and mussels as well.

At 500 m/yd, you will reach a trail junction and the first interpretive panel, which profiles St. Marys Bay and its high tides. Two benches also permit you to sit and enjoy the view. Continue along the water's edge. You will notice the interior part of the loop, actually coming to within 10 m/yd of it. At 1.6 km (1 mi), you will reach the tip of Pointe à Major, another interpretive panel, and more benches. To your right, you can see almost to the Seawall at Rossway near Digby, to your left the length of Long Island and beyond. The steeple of the massive church at Church Point is clearly visible, as is the huge stone church at St. Bernard.

You are standing on the largest gravel beach deposit in the Bay of Fundy. The point is named after Colonel Anselm Doucette, who, for some reason, was affectionately known as "Major" Doucette. His colonial house, which dates back to 1785, still overlooks the point on the ridge behind. One fascinating feature of the point is the structure of the ridges of gravel, which look like ocean waves.

At 2 km (1.5 mi), the trail intersects a road and turns left, reaching a Provincial Historical Site 300 m/yd later. Marked with a bronze plaque, it includes a small shrine and a cemetery surrounded by a white picket fence. This was the location of the first Mass held in Clare, on September 8, 1769, and, in 1774, it became the first blessed Acadian cemetery.

From here, the path returns, staying inland and crossing two small bridges over water passages. An extensive boardwalk skirts the edge of a wetland, and an alternate entrance for the community climbs the hill next to the Tasti-Freeze. At approximately 3.5 km (2.25 mi), you reach a trail junction; continue on the boardwalk to extend your walk another 200 m/yd bordering the wetlands, or turn left to the beach and your start.

Cautionary Notes:

Balancing Rock: The hillside is very steep. People unaccustomed to climbing should be prepared to go slowly and take frequent rests.

Sentier Piau: On stormy days Pointe à Major is completely exposed to the high winds and spray. I expect this might be more invigorating than dangerous, but at times it might be unpleasant.

Cellphone Reception: Adequate reception on both trails.

Shorebirds

Roger Tory Peterson (PMNL, GNL)

Anyone walking on one of Nova Scotia's beaches will invariably sight flocks of sparrow-sized birds apparently engaged in some sort of game with the ocean. Skittering rapidly across the sand, they advance or retreat up and down the beach just ahead of the leading edge of the waves. This is because their main diet is composed of mud-flat invertebrates, such as the small worm *Heteromastus filiformis*, which is found only in the intertidal zone. The most common species, semipalmated sandpipers and semipalmated plovers, prefer the mud shrimp of the Bay of Fundy to the Atlantic Coastline's offerings.

Dozens of varieties can be found along the coastline, especially during the fall migration period of July to September. Some, such as the whimbrel, are crow-sized, and minute variations of beak or leg colouring are often all that distinguish the various species.

Belleisle Marsh / Mickey Hill

Length: 3.5 km (2.25 mi) rtn
(Belleisle Marsh)
2 km (1.5 mi) rtn
(Mickey Hill)

Hiking Time: 1 hr

Type of Trail: gravelled treadway,
boardwalk, natural surfaces,
dirt road

Uses: hiking, cross-country
skiing

Facilities: interpretive panels
(Belleisle Marsh)
garbage cans, outhouses,
benches, tables, water, interpretive panels
(Mickey Hill)

Gov't Topo Map:
Bridgetown 21 A/14
(Belleisle Marsh)
Milford 21 A/11 (Mickey Hill)

Rating (1-5): 1

Trailhead GPS Reference:
N 44° 47' 39.3" W 65° 24' 03.2"
(Belleisle Marsh)
N 44° 39' 59.9" W 65° 27' 40.4"
(Mickey Hill)

Purple loosestrife in Bellisle Marsh. MH

itor Parking area is 1 km (.6 mi) on
the right.

Mickey Hill: From Annapolis Royal,
drive southwest on Highway 8 for
10.5 km (6.5 mi). A large sign indicates trailhead parking on the left.

Access Information:

Belleisle Marsh: From Annapolis
Royal, drive northeast on Highway 1
for 13 km (8 mi). Watch for the sign
for Little Brook Road. Continue on
Highway 1 for 400 m/yd, turning right
onto an unnamed dirt road. The vis-

Introduction:

Belleisle Marsh: The Belleisle Marsh
Wildlife Management Area was ini-
tiated in 1990 as part of the North
America Waterfowl Management
Plan. The Province purchased 283 ha
(700 acres) of the broad low marsh to

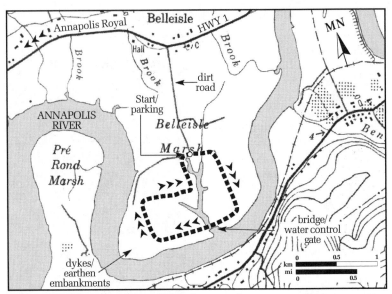

Belleisle Marsh

be protected as waterfowl habitat. However, located on the rich alluvial plain of the Annapolis River, Belleisle Marsh includes some of the most productive agricultural land in Nova Scotia. So, 69 ha (171 acres) were left as wetlands and 135 ha (333 acres) are being managed as upland habitat, but 79 ha (196 acres) are being used for agricultural production.

Mickey Hill: The land that makes up the Mickey Hill Pocket Wilderness belongs to Bowater Mersey Paper Company Ltd. There is a map of the trail posted at the parking lot and the gravel trail includes a picnic area and freshwater beach. There are in-

terpretative sites and a boardwalk through a marsh as well as a suspension bridge and a treetop lookout. More than 160 ha (400 acres) of the land bordering Lambs Lake was designated a conservation area by Bowater Mersey in 1994.

The Bowater Forest Recreation Program consists of four forest recreation areas open to visitors year-round: Old Annapolis Hiking Trail, Mickey Hill Pocket Wilderness, Port L'Hebert Pocket Wilderness, and Pine Grove. These sites include hiking trails, cross-country ski trails, and a waterfowl sanctuary. Bowater annually commits substantial funds for maintenance of the sites, and, in 1997,

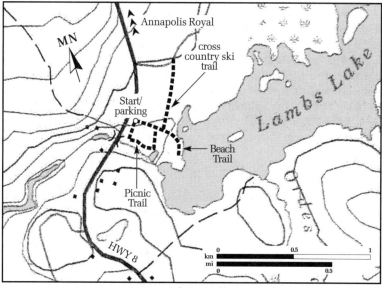

Mickey Hill

won a Nova Scotia Environment Award for its efforts.

Trail Description:

Belleisle Marsh: This is a short, flat walk around a broad grassy marshland that is a wonderful birdwatching location. At the parking area, a large interpretive panel features a good map of the small peninsula, which looks almost like a thumb pressing into the Annapolis River, forcing the water to flow around it. One direction is as good as the other, as this is a loop, but let us turn left and follow the grass surfaced road east.

The path turns south after only 300 m/yd, crossing a small brook that in the late summer is choked with thick vegetation. Expect ducks and even herons to be lurking in the shallow watercourse. The route continues for 750 m/yd until it comes to a dike separating the shallow marsh from the river. The hills of South Mountain on the far bank appear quite close, and, if you climb to the top of the dike, you can see the abandoned rail line on the opposite shore, barely 300 m/yd away. The view along the river is extensive, the lines of North and South Mountains disappearing into the distance in both directions.

Turning west, 300 m/yd later the trail comes to a bridge over a substantial brook that bisects the marshlands. This bridge is also a control mechanism to regulate the flow of water between the river and the marshlands. The path continues west for a further 700 m/yd before it turns north and away from the marsh's perimeter.

The treadway of the next section is more grass-covered and stays mostly in the interior of the protected area. Expect quite a bit of birdlife in the surrounding bushes and grasses. At the next junction, 2.5 km (1.5 mi) into the walk, turn either left or right, because both will connect again just before reaching the parking area. If you take the left, or slightly longer route, you will have walked 3.5 km (2.25 mi) by the time you finish your hike.

Mickey Hill: The parking area is quite developed, with a large kiosk in the centre providing a map of the path system and natural history information. From the right side of the parking area, the Picnic Trail heads directly to an area of tables, boardwalk, and bridges beside a lovely stream. Huge granite outcroppings dominate, making you feel as if you are in the middle of a rock garden. Large pine and spruce spring from between the boulders, spreading a canopy high overhead.

The footpath works upstream, crossing over a suspended bridge, and traces the boundary of a marshy cove. Frequent interpretive panels help explain the features of this beautiful little area. At the head of the marsh, the Picnic Trail ends when it meets the Beach Trail. Turn right, and follow this path for 200 m/yd to a lovely sandy area on the shore of Lambs Lake. Just beyond the junction, the Beach Trail intersects an abandoned road, to the left, that provides an added 4 km (2.5 mi), one way, of pathway. This road is most often used for cross-country skiing.

From the beach, return to the parking area, having hiked barely 2 km (1.25 mi). This walk is suitable for anyone, especially young families.

Cautionary Notes: You must yield to farm equipment on the road to Belleisle Marsh.

Hunting is permitted on some of these lands. Consult with the Department of Natural Resources in the fall for dates for various hunting seasons.

Cellphone Reception: Adequate reception on Belleisle Marsh. Inadequate reception available at Mickey Hill.

Further Information: Bowater Mersey produces a pamphlet outlining the features of its Pocket Wildernesses.

Blomidon Provincial Park

Length: 13 km (8 mi) rtn
Hiking Time: 4-5 hr
Type of Trail: walking paths,
    fields
Uses: hiking
Facilities: outhouses, water,
    picnic tables, camping,
    firewood, garbage cans,
    showers, playground
Gov't Topo Map:
    Parrsboro 21 H/8
Rating (1-5): 3
Trailhead GPS Reference:
    N 45° 15' 25.9" W 64° 21' 04.9"

Access Information: From Highway
101, take Exit 11 north to the junction with Highway 1 and Highway
358. Follow Highway 358 to Canning
then take the Pereau Road until you
run out of pavement. The total distance from Highway 101 is 25 km
(15.5 mi). You can park in the lot at
the bottom of the hill or continue on
the road up the hill to a lot at the
top, which reduces both the hiking
distance and the degree of difficulty.

Introduction: Blomidon Provincial
Park is positioned on the top of a massive 183 m (600 ft) cliff overlooking
the Minas Basin and dominating
the entire skyline. The brick red of
the sandstone hillside is mirrored in
the broad mud flats that are exposed

*Blomidon Provincial Park, last lookoff with
Parrsboro in the distance.* MH

by the retreat of the highest tides in
the world, an elevation change between tides of 12 m/yd. The views of
the Minas Basin and the Parrsboro
shores are breathtaking, and one of the
area's principal visitors' attractions.
The 759 ha (1,875 acres) park includes
72 campsites, and picnic areas both
at the top and at the bottom of the hill.
Blomidon Prov-incial Park was established in 1965.

Trail Description: From the lower
parking lot, follow the road uphill
looking for signs on your left mark-

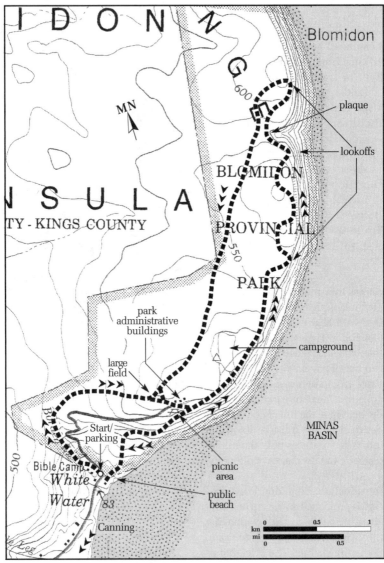

Blomidon Provincial Park

ing the entrance to the Borden Brook Trail. Rectangular red metal flashes denote the path; in the other direction, the flashes are yellow. At a junction just inside the woods, straight ahead takes you to a series of small waterfalls, while turning left sends you up the steep hillside along a narrow path, your toughest climb of the trek. You quickly reach the top of the ridge on an old road. Turn right and follow the road across the bridge over Borden Brook, reentering the woods to your left. In the spring and summer look for redstarts and northern parula warblers in the alders here. Moving on, you once again join an old road for a few paces. Be cautious at the next junction. Your trail, marked by red-tipped posts goes right. Continuing straight will send you on the road to Scots Bay, many difficult kilometres distant.

The trail reaches a large field originally cleared by the New England settlers who farmed this land in the 1770s. Leave the path, and cross over the field until you find either the administration building or the upper picnic area, visible from the top of the hill in the middle of the field. Rejoin the trail near the camping area, where cliff access is restricted by a long fence. You are now on the Joudrey Trail. Skirting through a forest of maple, birch, and beech, the trail rounds a small pond and arrives at the first lookoff. The cliffs of Five Islands Provincial Park across Minas Basin are prominent, and, on a clear day, you can almost spot Truro in the distance.

The trail continues along a well-worn route through open woods near the cliff edge. The next lookoff along Cape Blomidon's cliffs faces Parrsboro, after which the trail descends into a ravine to a bridge at Indian Springs Brook, the site of a plaque commemorating a land donation by Mr. Joudrey. The Lookoff Trail continues through mature spruce stands to a final cliffside panorama, two viewing areas facing northeast and southeast.

The return trip follows the Woodland Trail. Just outside the western boundary of the park, the trail passes a rapidly regenerating clear-cut area. Partridge sightings are common along this section. After about 3 km (2 mi), the path widens and becomes gravel-covered. You are near the campground, to your left, and its small interpretive trail. Continue straight, crossing the road to the group campsite, until you again reach the large field. Turn left across the field to reach the picnic area and regain the trail at its far south end. Your path descends now, with little more than 1 km (.5 mi) of walking remaining.

Yellow flashes sign your steeply dropping route, with stairs providing assistance at rough sections. Near the bottom the path becomes a broad grassy field, but beware of the electrified fence on your right, especially if walking with children. If you are fortunate, it will be low tide, and you will enjoy a view of almost 500 m/yd of mud flats extending from beneath high sandstone cliffs. Continue through the field until you spot the staircase leading you back to the lower parking lot and your car.

Cautionary Notes: Much of the hike parallels a high, very steep, and actively eroding cliff. Exercise extreme caution near lookoffs, and never venture beyond fences or other barriers.

The reddish flowers of the purple trillium cover the forest floor in the spring. This is a locally rare plant and should never be picked.

Cellphone Reception: Adequate throughout.

Further Information: A brochure about Blomidon Park can be obtained by contacting the Department of Natural Resources.

The local tourism association prints a brochure about hiking in Glooscap country. It can be picked up at local tourist bureaus.

Spruce

The three native species of spruce and one European introduction, the Norway spruce, make up more than 50% of the boreal forest of Nova Scotia and are the primary source of pulp for the paper industry.

White spruce, often found in pure stands reclaiming abandoned farmland, is also the dominant tree on the Atlantic coastline because of its tolerance of high salt concentrations. The Mi'kmaq used its roots for sewing birch bark on canoes.

Black, or bog, spruce grows in poorly drained areas. Children used to chew its hardened resin as gum and spruce beer was once a remedy for scurvy. Fishers prefer its wood for lobster traps.

The red spruce, the most common softwood and used extensively for pulpwood and boat-building, is the provincial tree. It frequently hybridizes with black spruce.

Delaps Cove

Length: 9.5 km (6 mi) rtn
Hiking Time: 2-3 hr
Type of Trail: dirt road, walking paths
Uses: hiking, mountain biking, cross-country skiing
Facilities: outhouses, picnic tables, benches
Gov't Topo Map: Digby 21 A/12, Granville Ferry 21 A/13
Rating (1-5): 2
Trailhead GPS Reference:
    N 44° 45' 39.2" W 65° 38' 57.4"

Delaps Cove. MH

Access Information: From Annapolis Royal, follow Highway 1 across the causeway to Granville Ferry. Turn onto Parkers Cove Road heading towards the Bay of Fundy. Turn left at the intersection at the shoreline towards Delaps Cove, and continue until the pavement ends. The total distance from Annapolis Royal is 22 km (13.75 mi). A road sign directs you left on a steep dirt road for 2 km (1.25 mi) ending in the parking lot.

Introduction: Situated on the other side of North Mountain from the county seat at Annapolis Royal, exposed to the harsher weather of the Bay of Fundy, and located on infertile basalt rock, Delaps Cove was typical of the poor areas granted to Black Loyalist immigrants. The 1871 census listed 70 inhabitants, with all the families but one being black. Some managed to become fairly prosperous; James Francis owned 125 acres of land, 12 sheep, 2 oxen, a house, a barn, and a boat. The majority was not so fortunate. Just one house remains occupied today, and only the rock walls, apple trees, and foundations remain of this former community.

The Municipality of Annapolis County opened this trail in 1985. There is much to see on this walk: the remains of the former settlement, a waterfall, interesting plant life, and the Bay of Fundy itself.

Trail Description: A large interpretive display at the trailhead contains

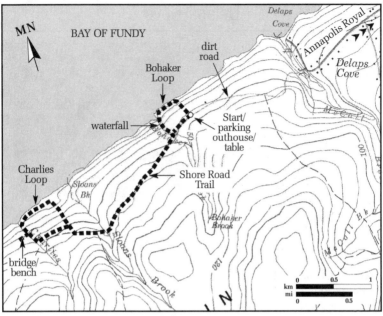

Delaps Cove

a map of the path network, and there are outhouses at the parking lot. You will also find a guest book waiting for your signature. Turn right, the 2.2 km (1.5 mi) Bohaker Loop quickly takes you downhill to the ocean and an interpretive sign describing tides. Following the coastline, the trail overlooks exposed basalt ridges running from the forest edge into the water. In some places huge rectangular boulders stand separate, eroded by the constant tidal action. After 400 m/yd you reach Bohaker Brook, where a small cliff-lined cove has been etched into the basalt, and the

waves have jammed it with driftwood. At the back of the hollow is 13 m (43 ft) Bohaker Falls. The trail heads inland now, although a side path crosses the brook, ending in a lookoff at the top of the waterfall, and provides one of the nicest views of the hike.

Leaving the coast, you move inland through lovely spruce and balsam fir stands paralleling the brook. Well-constructed bridges lead you to the other side. At a junction, turn left to return to the parking lot, crossing an impressive old stone wall en route, or head right towards the Shore Road and the Charlies Loop. In 300 m/yd, the right-hand path connects to the Shore Road, the remains of a former highway that used to run the length of North Mountain. There is little shade along this 2.7 km (1.75 mi) stretch, so wear a hat and carry lots of water on hot, sunny summer days. As the trail is not ditched, however, expect it to be wet in spring and fall. Few landmarks are available, except the descent to the crossing of Sloans Brook at about 2 km (1.25 mi).

One small sign marks the entrance to the 1.9 km (1.25 mi) Charlies Loop; pay attention. Goldenthread, a popular folk remedy for mouth pain, grows abundantly among long beech fern, bracken fern, and bunchberries. Several side trails take you to the water's edge with the last spur featuring an observation deck overlooking Charlies Cove and the coastline towards Digby Gut. On a clear day you should sight the Digby-Saint John ferry. Following the brook, you encounter the foundation of the Pomp household (see interpretive panel), and, just beyond that, a second, smaller site.

Anyone wanting a rest, or a few moments of contemplation, should take the side trail across Charlies Brook. Only 100 m/yd long, it descends into the steep, narrow ravine to a bench beside and above the cascading waters enfolded by mature softwoods, a perfect place for a sandwich or even a nap. From here, return to the park-ing lot via the Shore Road Trail, about 3 km (2 mi).

Cautionary Notes: Shore Road is used by ATVs. Please listen for them, and be prepared to move out of the way.

Expect to encounter wood ticks from April to July.

Hunters use this area. Seasons differ from year to year and for different species. Contact the Department of Natural Resources for detailed information. Be sure to wear hunter orange in the fall.

Cellphone Reception: Adequate throughout.

Further Information: The Municipality of Annapolis County offers a variety of pamphlets and guides for the Delaps Cove Trail.

Gaspereau River

Length: 9 km (5.5 mi) return
Hiking Time: 2-3 hr
Type of Trail: footpaths
Uses: hiking
Facilities: none
Gov't Topo Map: Wolfville 21 H/1
Rating (1-5): 2
Trailhead GPS Reference:
   N 45° 02' 54.4" W 64° 24' 53.7"

Access Information: Take Exit 11 off Highway 101 and turn uphill toward the Old Orchard Inn. Drive to the intersection at the Ridge Road, 1.5 km (1 mi) from Highway 101. Turn right, and drive 2.5 km (1.25 mi) to the village of White Rock. Turn right at the first stop sign, and left at the next sign less than 100 m/yd later. You are heading toward Black River. About 500 m/yd later, the road crosses a bridge; park on the left on the far side of the river.

Introduction: Although it's been more than 100 years since it has been used as a road, the Gaspereau River Trail follows an old cart track up a narrow river gorge in the Gaspereau Valley, in Kings County. The Gaspereau Valley runs roughly parallel to the Annapolis Valley but is part of the South Mountain Slope Unit of the Atlantic Interior Terrestrial Theme Region.

This is a pleasant hike up a small stream in a fairly narrow valley. I have provided details up to the point where the path crosses the river, although it continues many kilometres upstream. As it becomes increasingly less distinct, and, because there is no bridge and the river must be forded most of the year, I have ended the hike here.

Trail Description: The trail begins on the far side of the bridge on the opposite side of the road. At first, it may be difficult to find, but, as soon as you are past a minor obstacle of a fallen tree, your route becomes a distinct footpath running along the slope of the hill beside the river. The river itself is fairly wide and shallow, especially in the summer and fall. The hill slope on your right is quite steep and high. Expect to find kingfishers, eagles, and herons in the little pools in the bends in the stream.

About 400 m/yd along you will cross a very tiny bridge over a deep runoff channel from the hillside. The woods are fairly thick and you do not have much of a view until you climb a little slate ridge slightly more than 1 km (.6 mi) into the hike. There is no signage, and there are no large structures, but the bridging has been replaced and stone walkways have been placed in many of the wet areas. At times, the pathway is wide

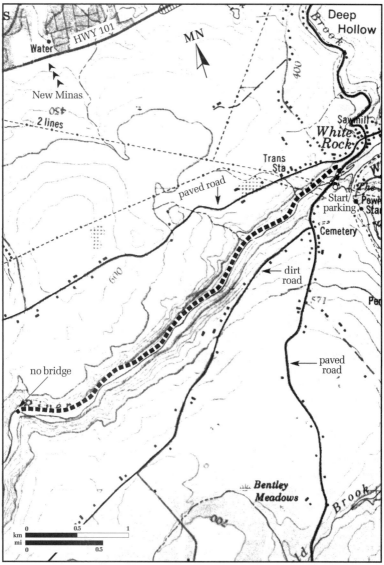

Gaspereau River

enough for two to walk side-by-side, and there is evidence that recent dead-fall has been removed from the path.

Some of the trees throughout this section are quite old, and the tread-way has been built up with slate on the streamside. Small bridges at 1.5 km (1 mi) and 2.5 km (1.5 mi) permit you to cross tiny streams without getting your feet wet. Beyond the second bridge, the valley widens some-what and the trail stays close to the hillside while the stream meanders toward the far slope. This is a wonderful area of young hardwood, filtering the sunlight into a soft green glow under its leafy canopy.

The path narrows again after a few hundred metres/yards, with occasional slate outcroppings requiring climbs to traverse. After about 3.75 km (2.25 mi) into the walk, the valley has distinctly begun to narrow, with the ridges closing in on both banks. The path has become a foot-track, the stream is reduced to barely 3 m/yd wide, and you are required to climb more often.

At 4.5 km (2.75 mi), the trail ends at the stream by a large granite rock. Further travel on the same bank is difficult, because large deadfall comes right to the edge of the water and the slope is steep and rocky. There is some evidence that the route may continue on the far bank, but there is no bridge and it is not possible to proceed without fording. Sit here for a time on the large granite rock in the river and enjoy your lunch. Then return to your car along the same path.

Cautionary Notes: GPS does not work in many spots under the thick vegetation canopy.

Hunting is permitted in many of the surrounding woods.

Cellphone Reception: Cell phones will not work in the gorge. Reception is minimal at the trailhead.

Moses Mountain

Length: 7.5 km (4.75 mi) rtn
Hiking Time: 2-3 hr
Type of Trail: gravel road, woods road
Uses: hiking, biking, cross-country skiing
Facilities: none
Gov't Topo Map:
 Windsor 21 A/16
Rating (1-5): 3
Trailhead GPS Reference:
 N 44° 53' 16.5" W 64° 12' 51.2"

Access Information: Turn off Highway 101 at Exit 5, Route 14, approximately 65 km (40 mi) from Halifax. Drive toward Chester, roughly 16 km (10 mi), and turn off the highway onto a dirt road on your right, the Eastern Valley Hydro System Avon #2 Hydro Plant. A gate crosses the road almost immediately. Park anywhere near here, but do not block the road.

Introduction: Scattered throughout Nova Scotia is a considerable network of hydro dams, each generating small amounts of power. Many of these dams are not too far from a paved road, and the access roads for the Nova Scotia Power Corporation make pleasant, and fairly easy walking, hikes for a Sunday morning or afternoon. In Hants County, far up the Avon River, past the fertile fields of Windsor Forks and Upper Falmouth, but abutting Highway 14, is the network of the Eastern Valley Hydro System Avon #2 Hydro Plant.

This is the kind of walk perfect for

MacDonald Pond and Dam, Moses Mountain. MH

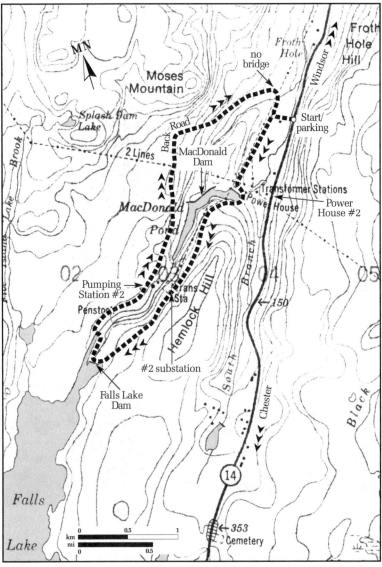

MN

Moses
Mountain

Froth
Hole

Froth
Hole
Hill

no
bridge

Windsor

Start/
parking

Splash Dam
Lake

Back Road

2 Lines

MacDonald
Dam

Transformer Stations

MacDonald
Pond

Power House

Power
House #2

Pumping
Station #2

Trans
Sta

Penstock

Hemlock Hill

South Branch

←150'

#2 substation

Falls Lake
Dam

Chester

Black

14

Falls
Lake

353
Cemetery

km 0   0.5   1
mi 0   0.5

Moses Mountain

a relaxed afternoon out of doors. The path is wide and even, the hills are not too steep, although there is some climb. Falls Lake is quite attractive, as is the small diversion channel re-routing the Avon River into the pen-stock. The view of Moses Mountain, Froth Hole Hill, and the Transformer Station from the power lines on the Back Road is quite impressive, as is the view of the cliffs along the east-ern bank of the Avon viewed from the Back Road above #2 Power House.

Trail Description: The first several kilometres follow gravel roads main-tained by the NSPC for their equip-ment. These are high-quality, and make easy walking. There is actually a fair amount of climbing involved, more than 91 m (300 ft) vertically from the parking area to Falls Lake Dam. However, while the ascent is fairly steady, the grade is not extreme, so most will find the effort invigorating rather than exhausting. Turn left at the gate and follow the wide grav-elled road towards Falls Lake Dam. You begin to climb immediately and, at 900 m/yd, you will reach MacDon-ald Pond and a junction with a path to MacDonald Dam, which is to the right. Turn left instead, and work your way around the water over an earthen embankment.

On the far side of the pond, the path begins to climb again, working its way up the slopes of Hemlock Hill. You might find that name odd, since the majority of the trees on the slopes are hardwoods. At 1.7 km (1 mi), a path steeply descends the hillside to your right. This continues for 500 m/yd and ends at an old pow-er station on the bank of the original route of the river. This makes an in-teresting side trip. On the main route, another 300 m/yd uphill and you will reach the former site of #2 sub-station, and, 200 m/yd further, a path to your left will take you to the base of a communication tower at the height of Hemlock Hill. Unfortunate-ly, there is no view.

At 2.3 km (1.5 mi), the trail finally stops climbing and you now walk downhill the remaining 900 m/yd to Falls Lake and the dam there. This has recently been extensively rebuilt, and an excellent fenced walkway is available that permits access to the far side. Swallows fill the air around Falls Lake Dam, and look for an osprey nest on a nearby power pole. The gorge is rocky from the original path of the river, and there is quite a drop from dam level.

On the far side, your path turns right and becomes an older road sur-face, much narrower with more shade from encroaching trees. It follows the diverted path of the stream until that enters a wide tube called a "penstock." The trail enters young woods, pre-dominantly birch and beech, and these continue for the remainder of your hike. About 600 m/yd past Falls Lake, an open area provides a view of impressive cliffs on the far wall of the gorge, and, 300 m/yd later, the trail reaches Pumping Station #2, where there are steep cliffs and no railings.

The path narrows and descends steeply to cross a small creek at 4.5 km (2.75 mi). The next 500 m/yd is the steepest climb of the day, and, 100 m/yd after the crest, you reach an open space where power lines cross high overhead. It is almost all down-hill from here, down the slope of Moses Mountain through a beautiful canopy of trees. At 7 km (4.5 mi), the path turns right and crosses the shallow Avon River. There is no bridge, so the narrow stream must be forded. In the summer I could hop from rock to rock without wetting my feet. Turn right, and, 200 m/yd later, you return to the gate and your car.

Cautionary Notes: Wood ticks are active from April to July.

Do not swim in Falls Lake near the dam or MacDonald Pond. Be extremely cautious near the cliffs and fording the river.

Cellphone Reception: Adequate reception, except in the final kilometre (.6 mi) and near the trailhead, where it may be inadequate.

Future Plans: The Hants County Trails Association is negotiating with the Nova Scotia Power Corporation to provide better signage on the route.

Osprey

Roger Tory Peterson (PMNL, GNL)

Look closely at that crow-sized bird circling lazily overhead. If the wings are heavily banded with white, it is likely that it is an osprey, the official bird of Nova Scotia. Once almost exterminated from the East Coast by the effects of insecticide pollution, it has made a remarkable comeback and now is a common sight in shallow bays, estuaries, and lakes. One enterprising early morning bird regularly picks up its breakfast from the pond at the Public Gardens in downtown Halifax!

The diet of these beautiful summer residents is almost exclusively fish. Anyone who has ever seen one plunge from 30 m (100 ft) into the water in an explosion of spray, only to emerge with its victim firmly grasped in its talons, will probably want to throw away their own fishing rod.

Mount Uniacke Museum

Length: 12 km (7.5 mi)
  combination
Hiking Time: 4-5 hr
Type of Trail: former road,
  walking paths
Uses: hiking, cross-country skiing
Facilities: picnic tables, benches,
  outhouses, garbage cans,
  interpretive panels
Gov't Topo Map:
  Middle Sackville 11 D/13
Rating (1-5): 3
Trailhead GPS Reference:
  N 44° 54' 06.7" W 63° 50' 39.6"

Access Information: Starting in the Halifax – Dartmouth metro area, take Highway 101 towards the Annapolis Valley for 15 km (9.5 mi) until you reach Exit 3. From Exit 3, turn left (west) on Highway 1 and drive 9 km (5.5 mi) through the village of Mount Uniacke. The estate entrance is on the left (south) side of road, well signed. Parking on the estate grounds requires a short drive on the dirt road.

Introduction: Work began on this trail in late 1994, with completion of the first phase, including most of the trails, in June of 1995. Uniacke Estate is a great place to visit on a weekend to stretch your legs, and their walking routes are a fine addition to Nova Scotia's trail network.

Trail Description: Several walking opportunities begin from the parking lot. An interpretive panel located next to the estate house contains a map showing the trail network. The walks vary in difficulty with all fitness levels being accommodated, including a wheelchair-accessible walk.

From the parking lot, walk behind the main estate building and follow the wide, gravelled path as it leads into a field past several buildings. There is a formal trailhead, where you turn left and walk to the shoreline of Uniacke Lake, which was once known as Lake Martha. The path heads in both directions. Turn left and continue southeasterly along its shore until you reach the bridge crossing the brook draining Norman Lake. This portion, named the Lake Martha Trail, features interpretive panels and benches and is the easiest walking of the trail. A short path heads left and connects to the entrance road, permitting a 500 m/yd return loop that is wheelchair-accessible. Those interested may continue straight on the path along the lakeshore, passing through mixed forest to loop across the top of a drumlin and the remains of old fields, a total distance 1.5 km (1 mi). This path also connects to a trailhead outside the estate grounds on Murphy Lake, be-

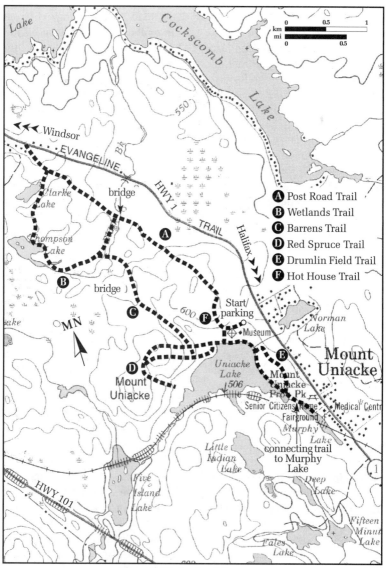

A Post Road Trail
B Wetlands Trail
C Barrens Trail
D Red Spruce Trail
E Drumlin Field Trail
F Hot House Trail

Mount Uniacke Museum

hind the community firehall, adding almost another 1 km (.6 mi)

If, from the lakeshore, one turns right (northwest), the path heads into the interior toward the hills overlooking Uniacke Lake. Somewhat more challenging walking than the Drumlin Field Trail, the Red Spruce Trail features a section passing through magnificent mature spruce stands and crossing through rocky terrain over several hills. Bridges are rudimentary, often just logs thrown across wet areas and the treadway is natural surface. A return trip of more than 2 km (1.25 mi), this branch revisits the same route to the lake.

Barrens Trail: Barely 300 m/yd from the start of this path, the Barrens Trail cuts into the interior. Well signed, the path gently climbs through thick softwoods and many wet areas for the first 700 m/yd before the ground becomes rockier and the pathway more rugged. About 600 m/yd later, you will pass through a large fire barrens. The path descends into another barrens, crossing a stream over a narrow one-person bridge at 1.6 km (1 mi). Up the hill, on the other side, the Barrens Trail joins the Wetlands Trail. Turning left means completing at least an additional 5 km (3 mi) to return to the parking area; turning right requires a less than 3 km (2 mi) hike.

Post Road Trail: Leading right from the trailhead, the Hot House Trail loops around a small hill and connects to the Old Windsor Road, the Post Road Trail. One of Nova Scotia's two "Great Roads" required for movement of troops and cattle after the founding of Halifax, the Halifax – Windsor road featured weekly stage service by 1801, with mail and passenger service offered by 1815. Mount Uniacke, located halfway between the communities, made a convenient watering place. On the estate are nearly 3 km (2 mi) of the original alignment, including the #27 milestone. The Post Road Trail continues almost to the far end of the property, where the old track rejoins Highway 1, a 6 km (3.75 mi) return trip.

Wetlands Trail: A final trail, accessible only from the Barrens Trail and the further ends of the Post Road Trail, cuts into the interior of the estate in a loop taking it near two small lakes and a brook. The Wetlands Trail provides several opportunities to sit beside these water features. Perhaps 3 km (2 mi) long, this is the most remote and challenging walk on the estate. A narrow footpath over alternatively rocky and boggy ground, most people will find it requires good footwear. Combining the Wetlands Trail with the Post Road Trail and Barrens Trail produces a loop hike of at least 8 km (5 mi).

Cautionary Notes: Because of its proximity to swamp, stream, and bog, the Wetlands Trail will often be, well, wet. Be prepared for soggy footings, particularly in spring and after rains.

Cellphone Reception: Adequate in most places, but sometimes not in areas of especially thick vegetation.

Further Information: The Nova Scotia Museum produces a brochure about the Uniacke Estate. Contact their Public Information Officer. Public walks are regularly scheduled here by hiking clubs.

Richard John Uniacke

Born in Ireland in 1753, Richard John Uniacke established himself as a lawyer in Halifax in 1781, eventually becoming the Attorney-General of Nova Scotia in 1797. In 1786, Uniacke obtained his first property, a grant of 405 ha (1000 acres). Eventually acquiring, by 1819, consolidated holdings of 4589 ha (11,340 acres), Uniacke developed a working farm and built what has been described as "one of Canada's finest examples of colonial architecture . . . a grand country house in the Georgian tradition." Richard John died in his bed at Mount Uniacke in 1830.

In 1949, the remainder of the estate, approximately 930 ha (2300 acres), was sold by the family to the Province of Nova Scotia, and, in 1960, the property became part of the Nova Scotia Museum. Since 1951, the estate has been open to the public, with the main building being the principal attraction. Over the last several years, however, there has been a re-evaluation of the use of this extensive property, culminating in a new Landscape Management Plan in 1993. Under this ambitious multi-year strategy, the Uniacke Estate landscape will be restored to its condition of 150 years ago and protected as an important cultural resource. Increased access to the property will also be encouraged through recreational trail development.

Nictaux Falls

Length: 20 km (12.5 mi) rtn
Hiking time: 4-6 hr
Type of Trail: abandoned rail line
Uses: hiking, mountain biking, horseback riding, cross-country skiing
Facilities: none
Gov't Topo Map:
Bridgetown 21 A/14
Rating (1-5): 4 [distance]
Trailhead GPS Reference:
N 44° 54' 18.9" W 65° 01' 50.7"

Access Information: From Middleton, take Highway 10 approximately 5.5 km (3.5 mi) to Nictaux Falls. Watch for the snowmobile crossing sign, and park by the side of the road. Follow the former rail line on the left of the highway.

Introduction: In 1889, the Nova Scotia Central Railway offered service between Bridgewater and Middleton, which continued until the line was abandoned by Canadian National in 1984. Since that time, snowmobilers and ATV riders have increasingly used this corridor. Although the walk from Nictaux Falls as far as Alpena Rapids is fairly long, this is a relatively easy hike and many people should be able to complete it. The most difficult portion is at the start,

so the return will be much less challenging.

The section climbing the Nictaux River is extremely attractive. Erosion has carved a deep valley through the Ordovician slate bedrock of the South Mountain Foothills. The granite of the South Mountain Rolling Plain, which you will find around Alpena Rapids, is much more resistant to weathering.

Trail Description: The road and trail separate almost immediately, with the highway climbing the slope of the hillside while the gravel path heads into the beckoning gap of the Nictaux River gorge. Immediately the slope on the right climbs steeply to tower over the path and water seeps down the side onto the treadway. You will be able to hear cars on the road above you and the roar of Nictaux River to your left and below.

Unlike most former rail lines, the section from Nictaux Falls very noticeably climbs almost immediately. Hugging the hillside, the trail winds right and left around uncharacteristically tight curves. You might notice tiny Smiths Island in the river below, and, 750 m/yd later, you will cross a small bridge across a steep stream cascading down the almost vertical cut. Trees from the right bank bend overhead, providing shade on most

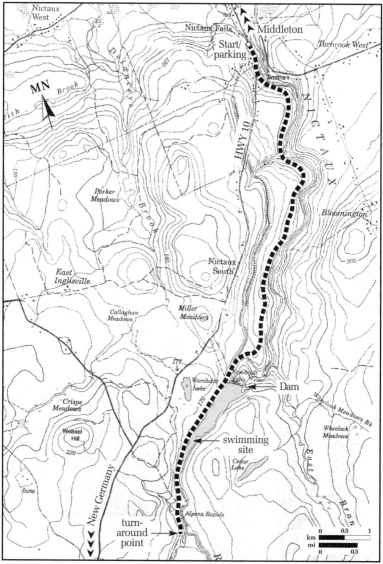

Nictaux Falls

days. The trees on both slopes are primarily hardwoods.

For the first 4 km (2.5 mi), the track is narrow and the climb substantial, more than 70 m (230 ft). Often the far side of the valley is visible when the slope is especially steep, and several times the trail skirts near the edge of the cliff. The following 3 km (2 mi) is more open, as the path nearly levels and becomes straighter. You pass through several narrow, wet rock cuts, and, at 6.5 km (4 mi), the vegetation gives way on the right. If you climb up, you will find the Nictaux Canal, and an easy, level walk back to the highway. Continuing another 500 m/yd along the trail, you reach Wamboldt Falls and a beautiful reservoir created by the large dam blocking the Nictaux River gorge. A walk is possible to the far end of the 500 m/yd embankment, and it is worthwhile not merely for the views of the reservoir, but also for its outflow at the far end of the dam. The small deep lake is long and narrow, and canoeists and kayakers are often found on its placid surface.

At the junction of the trail, dam, and Nictaux Canal, a dirt road heads right and uphill 1 km (.6 mi) to Highway 10. A small bridge passes over the sheer rock walls at the mouth of the canal, and for the next 2 km (1.5 mi) the trail follows the shore of the reservoir, staying quite close to the water's edge. Near the mouth of the Nictaux River, 1.5 km (1 mi) from the dam, you might notice a favourite swimming site of the local residents. ATV paths lead to the water to your left.

You may notice that the rocks are beginning to look different, for you are moving into the granites of the South Mountain. Continue another 1 km (.6 mi), and stop at the junction of Oakes Brook and Nictaux River. The surroundings are more rugged; erosion-resistant granite narrows the river and forces the stream to flow over and around the large rocks scattered throughout. The Alpena Rapids, on your left for the past several hundred metres/yards, is a restless, frothing cataract, especially during the spring runoff.

The adventurous could choose to follow the trail all the way to New Germany, 45 km (28 mi) further. However, for most I recommend that you turn back and retrace your route to Nictaux Falls.

Cautionary Notes: Wood ticks are active from April to July.

There may be many ATVs on the trail, and, although most areas have reasonably safe viewing distances, you should be aware that an encounter is a possibility.

Cellphone Reception: Inadequate reception throughout except near Wamboldt Falls on the dam.

Future Plans: The South Shore Annapolis Valley Recreational Trails Association is developing the abandoned rail line from New Germany through to Middleton as a shared-use recreational corridor.

Roxbury

Length: 18 km (11.25 mi) rtn
Hiking Time: 6-8 hr
Type of Trail: gravel road, woods road
Uses: hiking, biking, horseback riding, snowmobiling, ATV riding, cross-country skiing
Facilities: none
Gov't Topo Map: Bridgetown 21 A/14
Rating (1-5): 5 [distance, remoteness]
Trailhead GPS Reference: N 44° 51' 12.4" W 65° 11' 16.0"

Access Information: Turn off Highway 101 at Exit 19, approximately 165 km (103 mi) from Halifax. Head left about 3 km (2 mi) to Highway 1, turning left again into the village of Lawrencetown. Turn right onto Lawrencetown Lane and cross the Annapolis River to the junction with Highway 201. Turn right, and drive 4 km (2.5 mi) to West Paradise. Turn off the highway onto a dirt road on your left, at the "Roxbury Road" sign. Continue on the narrow lane 1 km (.6 mi), past the Lafarge Paradise Asphalt Pit. Park anywhere, and follow the old road uphill into the woods.

Introduction: Near the end of this old road you will discover some of the remains of an abandoned settlement that once contained as many as 135 people. It had its own school, two lumber mills, a grist mill, and numerous farms and orchards. All

Roxbury Road. MH

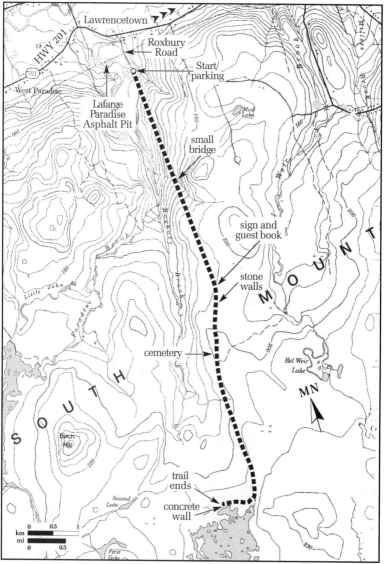

Roxbury

that remains of the settlement are graveyards, apple orchards, foundation depressions, stone walls, and one building. The Rosengreen House, built between 1860 and 1870, is the only remaining structure. Otherwise, white spruce has grown into the former fields, and a few hunting camps are the only signs of human activity. The only cleared land is near the Rosengreen, and this is rapidly growing over with each passing year.

A number of factors caused people to leave the area. The settlement survived on lumbering, but they were so successful that they depleted most of the resource in their area. The winter of 1895 was so severe that lumbering operations were cancelled due to deep snow, and the Great Fire of 1900 destroyed thousands of acres of woodland.

Trail Description: Where the road becomes too difficult for ordinary cars, you will find a small parking area. Your path continues along the rocky and eroded old road, which heads straight uphill. You will climb almost 150 m (500 ft) in this hike, most of it in the first 2.5 km (1.5 mi). At 1.5 km (1 mi), you will see considerable evidence of logging, and, at 2 km (1.5 mi), you cross a small brook on a bridge. After this, the climb becomes even steeper for the next 700 m/yd. At 2.25 km (1.5 mi), a logging road leads to the left; keep to the right path, even though it appears less distinct.

Once the path (nearly) levels, the vegetation includes much more hardwood, including some old maples. You may notice some painted mileage signs; unless you start walking from the entrance to the Lafarge asphalt pit, these will not conform to the distance you have walked. At 5 km (3 mi), you should sight a sign on a tree to your right welcoming you to "the Community of Roxbury." There will be a guest book there waiting for your signature. Another sign announces Roxbury, 1865, population 67. The stone fences of the community begin shortly afterward.

For the next 1.5 km (1 mi), the fences border both sides of the road, and small signs put up by the historical society indicate where wells and other former structures can be found. The field and ruins of the final house can be found on the left 500 m/yd later. At 5.8 km (3.6 mi), a sign directs you 200 m/yd down a side trail to the right to a family cemetery, definitely worth the walk. You will also notice that several hunting cabins are located in this area, maintained by descendants of the original settlers.

Beyond 6.5 km (4 mi), the cabins end and the track narrows considerably, suitable only for walking. The treadway is now almost completely grass-covered, and the vegetation grows thickly on both sides of the old road. Occasional stone wall remains can still be seen, and even a well sign or two. The path begins to descend into some of the most attractive forest of the hike. At 8 km (5 mi), you reach a junction. Turn right, and, within 200 m/yd, you will reach the shores of Paradise Lake. Along the shoreline, you will find the remains of campfires. This is a popular overnight destination for fishers, who can access the far shore on a road from West Dalhousie. The path ends at 8.5 km (5.5 mi), at a concrete retaining wall at the edge of the water. Return along the same route.

Cautionary Notes: Wood ticks are active from April to July.

Hunting is permitted in the woods bordering the trail. Wear hunter orange in the fall.

Cellphone Reception: Adequate reception for the first 7 km (4.5 mi). Beyond that, calls may not be made until you reach Paradise Lake.

Future Plans: The local historical society continues to restore some of the former homesteads.

Further Information: A local school teacher, David Whitman, has conducted research to find out as much about the former inhabitants as possible. He has written an article that is used in the local school curriculum, and can be occasionally convinced to lead a group up the bumpy, old road to the settlement remains.

Red Pine

Also known as the Norway pine, this tree is favoured for use as wharf and bridge pilings, power poles, and other purposes requiring a sturdy wood that is easily rot-proofed. Red pine was also used for ships' masts, and its heartwood was popular for ships' decks. Because of its commercial value, almost all the old growth trees in the province have been harvested.

NSMNH

Red pine adds one row of spreading branches each year for up to 350 years, and grows to heights of 24 m (80 ft). Its bark is reddish-brown with broad, flat, scaly plates. The needles come in bundles of two that are slender, whorled, and dark green year-round. Red pines prefer well-drained soils, particularly sand plains, and usually grow in mixed forests rather than pure stands.

The stairway to the beach at McGahey Brook, Cape Chignecto Provincial Park. MH

The beach at Refugee Cove, Cape Chignecto Provincial Park. Sea kayakers have pitched their tents questionably close to the high tide mark. MH

Amherst Point Migratory Bird Sanctuary

Length: 6 km (3.75 mi) rtn
Hiking Time: 1-2 hr
Type of Trail: walking paths
Uses: hiking, cross-country
  skiing
Facilities: interpretive panels,
  observation decks
Gov't Topo Map:
  Amherst 21 H/16
Rating (1-5): 1
Trailhead GPS Reference:
  N 45° 47' 50.1" W64° 15' 35.8"

Access Information: From Highway 104, take Exit 3 and drive southwest on the unnumbered road away from Amherst towards Nappan. Three kilometres (2 mi) past the Wandlyn Inn, a blue Canadian Wildlife Service sign on the left signals the entrance to the sanctuary's parking lot.

Introduction: Although relatively small, Amherst Point has much to offer. Designated a Migratory Bird Sanctuary in 1947 at the request of neighbouring landowners, it assumed its present size of 433 ha (1,070 a) in 1980. Together with the 600 ha (1,480 a) John Lusby Marsh, it makes up the Chignecto National Wildlife Area. A surprising variety of habitats lie within the sanctuary, but 66% of its area is open water, marsh, and bogs, or controlled water-level impoundments, an environment ideal for waterfowl.

The enclosed wetlands, specifically the impoundments created by the dikes and sluices built by Ducks Unlimited in the 1970s, are among the best waterfowl breeding grounds in Nova Scotia. More than 200 bird species have been observed at Amherst Point, which is a regular nesting site for regionally rare varieties such as gadwall, redhead, ruddy duck, virginia rail, common gallinule, and black tern. Gypsum deposits underlie the entire area, and, from 1935 to 1942, a commercial mine operated near the sanctuary.

Trail Description: Follow the road linking the parking lot to the highway, where there is a large sign including a map. A metal gate prevents vehicles from continuing, and the wide track leads 200 m/yd to a three-way junction at the top of a hill overlooking Laytons Lake. I recommend taking the left route, which follows the ridgeline along abandoned upland fields northeast for 400 m/yd.

No sign marks the right turn downhill, and a distinct path continues straight, but, at the first junction, descend toward the woods and Laytons Lake. A beautiful spruce canopy provides shade as the trail follows the water's edge; a solitary rough-

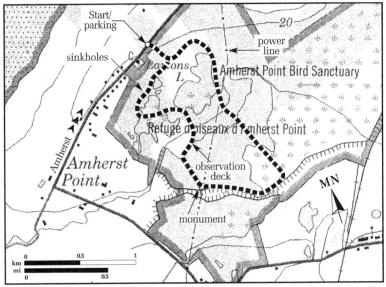

Amherst Point Migratory Bird Sanctuary

hewn bench looks out on a tiny cove. Following a ravine inland over a tiny bridge, the trail winds through woods, giving occasional views of Quarter Moon Lake. Rejoining Laytons Lake, the path follows its bank fairly closely until it connects to an abandoned rail line.

Turn left and follow this track to the power line. Continuing straight 300 m/yd leads to the dike separating impoundments 2a and 2b. Follow this, and, for the next 2 km (1.25 mi), you will walk on the narrow dirt causeways through the best waterfowl breeding areas. Birch trees shield you somewhat from the water on both sides, and for 800 m/yd the path

continues straight until it reaches the far shore. A dirt road heads over a hill directly ahead, but turn right and follow the dike system, soon a narrow unsheltered dirt track, for another 800 m/yd to the next junction. Here you will find a monument dedicating the Amherst Point II Bird Sanctuary and a bridge. On the far side is a "trail closed" sign, so turn right and continue only 400 m/yd back to drier and higher ground.

Continue a further 50 m/yd and find an observation deck tucked among the trees overlooking the marshes through which you just hiked. Walk 200 m/yd to another junction and one of the few directional signs in the sanctuary. Turn left here on the path separating forest and field. At the next junction, turn left again and almost immediately you encounter a small bridge spanning a brook. Laytons Lake is once again on your right. Just beyond the bridge is an X-junction; right leads up the hill 500 m/yd to the start, left goes into the field back towards the dikes. Continue straight instead, and, 300 m/yd later, find another observation deck overlooking The Cove on your left. Another bridge separates two ponds, and, on the other side, you re-enter the trees, gorgeous eastern hemlock, and encounter a trail junction and your second directional sign, guiding you right.

This is the only difficult walking of the hike. A handrail assists the climb up between steep-sided sink-holes. Note the sudden and dramatic change in the land. The trail traces the narrow crest of the ridges separating several depressions until reaching a small clearing called The Glen, where five interpretive panels describe the sanctuary's features. Completing the loop, only 200 m/yd farther along the path, is the initial junction on the top of the hill. Turn left again, after maybe one more look around, to return to the parking lot.

Cautionary Notes: Hunting is not permitted within Amherst Point. Be cautious in the fall and wear orange vests or hats.

Although ATV and snowmobile use is prohibited, both occur, especially underneath the power lines along the access road and the dikes.

Remember that this is a sanctuary, and that, at times throughout the year, you will encounter nests. Please resist the temptation to touch the eggs or interfere in any way. Do not take dogs into this area; they will certainly disturb nests.

Cellphone Reception: Adequate throughout.

Future Plans: In the near future, more walking routes will be cleared on the dikes.

Karst topography on the Fairmount Ridge Trail. MH

Karst Topography

When deposits of gypsum are in contact with the surface, it may cause the appearance of a strange landscape. Water easily dissolves the soft mineral. It may crumble and wash away, and subterranean channels are often formed with streams washing away more of the surrounding rock. Large caverns, such as Hays Cave in Hants County, can be created, and the whole area may become dangerous because it is underlaid with holes or channels.

In the Amherst Point Bird Sanctuary, conical depressions called "sinkholes," where the roof of a cavern has collapsed, are peppered throughout the site and create an unusual and rugged topography in places. You will also find several long, steep-sided gullies, the site of a collapsed stream channel. Amherst Point is one of the best sites in the province to find these sinkholes, the finest example located behind Kings Edgehill School in Windsor. You will also find this type of landscape on the Fairmont Ridge Trail near Antigonish.

Cape Chignecto Provincial Park

Length: 52 km (32.5 mi) rtn
Hiking Time: 3 days
Type of Trail: walking paths,
  dirt roads
Uses: hiking
Facilities: picnic tables, benches,
  garbage cans, outhouses,
  camping
Gov't Topo Map:
  Cape Chignecto 21 H/7
Rating (1-5): 5 [distance, rugged
  terrain]
Trailhead GPS Reference:
  N 45° 21' 01.1" W 64° 49' 28.9"

Access Information: From Parrsboro,
drive 46 km (29 mi) along Highway
209 to Advocate Harbour. On the far
side of town, turn left off 209 towards
West Advocate. Drive 3 km (2 mi) to
the Administrative Centre and the
parking area at the end of the paved
road at Red Rocks.

Introduction: Cape Chignecto Provincial Park is a 4200 ha (10,378 acres)
natural environment park located on
a dramatic coastal peninsula next to
the Bay of Fundy. The park offers
wilderness camping in secluded coves
and ravines by this remote shoreline. A wonderful walking trail takes
visitors along high cliffs and deep valleys. Cape Chignecto officially opened
July 25, 1998. This is both one of the

*Cape Chignecto Provincial Park, seen from
Christie Field.* MH

most difficult and one of the best
trails in Nova Scotia. Few prepared
footpaths are this long, and, when
completed from Cape Chignecto to
Apple River, it will be the longest in
any provincial park in Nova Scotia.

By British and Appalachian trail
standards, Cape Chignecto would only
rate as moderately difficult, or even
lower. The maximum elevation here
is only around 175 m (574 ft), whereas Mt. Katahdin in Baxter State Park
(Maine) climbs 1219 m (4000 ft) in 6
miles. I recommend taking three days

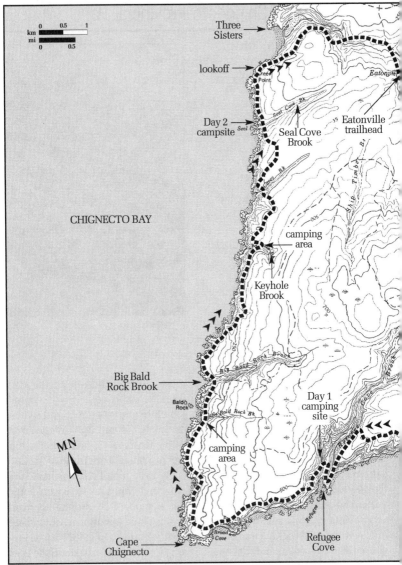

Three Sisters

lookoff

Green Point

Seal Cove Bk

Eatonville

Day 2 campsite

Seal Cove

Seal Cove Brook

Eatonville trailhead

CHIGNECTO BAY

Ship Timber Br.

camping area

Keyhole Brook

Big Bald Rock Brook

Bald Rock

Little Bald Rock Bk

Day 1 camping site

Cape Chignecto Br.

camping area

MN

Refugee Cove

Cape Chignecto

Broad Cove

Refugee Cove

km 0   0.5   1
mi 0   0.5

Cape Chignecto Provincial Park (Part 1)

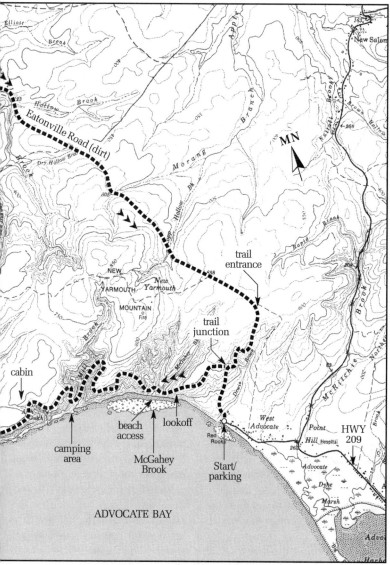

MN

Eatonville Road (dirt)

trail
entrance

NEW
YARMOUTH

New
Yarmouth

MOUNTAIN
Fire

trail
junction

cabin

beach
access

lookoff

McGahey
Brook

camping
area

Red
Rocks

West
Advocate

Point
Hill

Hospital

Start/
parking

Advocate

HWY
209

Dyke

Marsh

ADVOCATE BAY

Advo

Cape Chignecto Provincial Park (Part 2)

to hike the complete loop, and staying overnight if you wish to visit Refugee Cove and return. Camping and day-use fees must be paid at the Administrative Centre.

Trail Description: From Red Rocks, the route heads down toward the beach, but turns and starts uphill across Christie Field. You reach the forest 500 m/yd from the start, continuing along an old woods road marked with bright red metal flashes. The climb gets steeper now, until, at 600 m/yd, you notice a path branching to the right, marked by blue flashes. The main trail turns left, marked by red flashes, just ahead.

This is great trail, clearly marked with metal tags mounted on trees. Substantial clearing was necessary, as well as preparation of the treadway. Puncheons cross wet spots, and numerous small bridges reduce the difficulty of navigating the frequent deep narrow cuts in the hillside. For the first two kilometres you stay in woods until the first view station provides a magnificent look at Advocate Bay, the Minas Channel, Cape D'Or, and a sizable length of the Annapolis Valley coastline. Shortly after, the trail descends steeply into the first of the deep ravines slashing through the coastal cliffs.

McGahey Brook requires a set of constructed stairs and a bridge to reach, and immediately the trail climbs again regaining lost elevation. You will notice the junction for the McGahey Brook Loop just over the bridge; keep left. More stairwells aid the ascent, but expect the effort to work up a drenching sweat.

In similar fashion, you next drop into Mill Brook. Amazingly, the grade is steeper, and the effort required still greater. Perhaps the most riveting section of the trail is found in the climb on the other side of Mill Brook. At one point, a smooth rock face forms the wall for the narrow trail. Stones and tree roots have been used as stairs as the trail sharply scales the hillside, and the tops of nearby trees are often below the weary hiker. Your quads and calves will protest the sustained labour.

From the top the walk is much easier and almost level. You will notice one of the new backcountry cabins, and an outhouse, near the top of Arch Brook, 8 km (5 mi) from the start. At about 11.5 km (7.5 mi), another long, steep descent begins, ending at the mouth of Refugee Cove. The path turns right, and camping sites are 500 m/yd inland, above the high water mark. For most, this will be a good place to finish the first day's walk.

Day 2: After crossing Refugee Cove Brook on the new footbridge, the path steeply climbs again to French Lookoff, with excellent views of the coastal cliffs. Continuing through meadows and around Broad Cove, the path descends gradually until it reaches a signed junction at 5 km (3 mi). Turn left for 100 m/yd to reach Cape Chignecto – although there's not actually much of a view. Turning right, toward Spicers Cove, the main path becomes rougher, moving up and down the hillside as it gradually descends towards Stoney Beach and Little Bald Rock Brook, 3 km (2 mi) away. This is a fantastic coastline, with lookoffs built onto every headland. In some respects, the walking is more challenging on the first day, because the route is never level, constantly climbing and descending the rugged slopes.

At Little Bald Rock Brook you will find an outhouse and campsites next to a tiny brook in a narrow gorge, as you will at Big Bald Rock Brook, 2 km (1.25 mi) further. Anyone too energetic to stop at Refugee Cove might choose one of these isolated sites to spend the night. It is difficult to do justice to the next 12 km (7.5 mi), surely some of the finest coastal hiking in Nova Scotia. Rugged, scenic, and of breath-stealing beauty, this section is an unending succession of dramatic views. The climbs out of Keyhole Brook and Carey Brook are particularly memorable, and there is one inland climb that I will not forget either! The day's hike ends at the campsite at Seal Cove Brook, 22 km (13.75 mi) from Refugee Cove.

Day 3: After Seal Cove, the cliffs are perhaps only half as high, but impressive nevertheless. You cross some wonderful barrens for 1 km (.6 mi) before the path begins to curve away from the ocean. If you are lucky (it was foggy the day I hiked it), you will sight the famous Three Sisters, a row of tall, narrow basalt sea stacks. Once away from the water, you face one more challenging climb before the path descends to reach Eatonville Brook, where you cross a large, new bridge, about 4 km (2.5 mi) from Seal Cove. The path follows the river for another kilometre (.6 mi), then crosses again and climbs a long gentle hill through beautiful woods to reach the Eatonville Road perhaps 7 km (4.5 mi) from Seal Cove Brook.

The final 10 km (6 mi) is an easy walk following the Eatonville Road through the interior of Cape Chignecto. There are few views, and signage is limited to a few informal site names erected by volunteers. You finish your hike back at the parking area in Red Rocks, 18 km (11.25 mi) from the day's start. You can follow the back half of the McGahey Brook Loop near the walk-in campsites for the final few kilometres.

Cautionary Notes: Although it appears to be an easy walk to Refugee Cove along the coastline at low tide, never, ever attempt it. Extremely high tides, averaging 8 m (26 ft), wash far up the sheer unbroken cliffs, and it is very easy to become stranded.

Footing can be treacherous during wet weather. Make sure that you have sturdy footwear. A strong walking stick will be an asset.

Carry more water than usual; the thirst generated from the exertion of the long, steep climbs will require constant slaking.

Cellphone Reception: Adequate reception on most high ground, but minimal at sea level and none in the gorges or inland. Past Cape Chignecto, there is almost no reception.

Future Plans: A footpath from Eatonville to McGahey Brook is under construction and should open in 2002.

Sea Stacks

The ferocious tides of the Bay of Fundy constantly attack the shoreline between Economy and Cape Chignecto, and affect the two main soil groups of the area quite differently. Where soft sandstone is exposed, it erodes rapidly, creating wide tidal platforms. When volcanic basalt is present, high, steep-sided coastal cliffs are created where the more erosion-resistant rock, with its columnar structure, breaks apart more stubbornly.

Eventually, the relentless ocean wears away all the softer material, and only columns of basalt remain. These offshore pillars are known as sea stacks. Isle Haute, visible far out in the Bay of Fundy, the well-known Five Islands, near Economy Mountain, and the Three Sisters in Cape Chignecto Provincial Park are outstanding examples.

Further Information: www.capechignecto.net.

Once past Cape Chignecto, the trail often follows the edge of the cliff. MH

Cobequid Trail

Length: 13 km (8 mi) return
Hiking time: 3-4 hr
Type of Trail: abandoned rail line
Uses: hiking, biking
Facilities: water, benches, garbage
    cans, covered picnic tables,
    nearby stores
Gov't Topo Map: Truro 11 E/6
Rating (1-5): 2
Trailhead GPS Reference:
    N 45° 21' 31.5" W 63 17' 30.4"

Access Information: From Halifax, drive 100 km (62.5 mi) to Truro on Highway 102. Take Exit 13, turning right and driving about 1.5 km (1 mi) to Willow Street (Highway 2). Turn left at the streetlights, and drive less than 1 km to just past the hospital (on the right). The Green Gables and A&W complex are on the left. Turn left and park here.

Introduction: The Cobequid Trail is an initiative by the community to re-claim a portion of the former rail line that once connected Truro to Windsor, through the Kennetcook River Valley, and turn it into a recreational path. The municipality has acquired the land and has recently developed it into a multi-use path. Most of the length, from the Shubenacadie River to near Windsor, was sold to a private interest. Much of the remainder, from the Shubenacadie River to just outside Truro, was given to adjacent farmers. The town acquired the portion of rail line inside its limits.

The trail is typical abandoned rail bed: level, wide, and with no major climbs anywhere. The route is never more than a few hundred metres/yards from houses, except when it is out on the dikelands. Even there, housing is still within clear sight. Amenities such as stores can be found at various points along the trail.

The western section of the trail connects to the dikelands along the Salmon River near the Palliser Restaurant. This is a great place to watch the tidal bore where more than 10 km (6.25 mi) of dikes run in both directions. The maintenance roads run at their base, and the grassed slopes are easy walking on a fine, fall day. This is a great location for bird watching at this time of year: ducks, geese, and hawks are among the many species you should be able to find while on your walk. Ringed-neck pheasants are another common sight, especially in the grassy fields of the dikelands.

Trail Description: At present, the prepared treadway will take you from just behind the Community College (former Teacher's College), out into the dikelands of Lower Truro. It starts behind the Armour Trucking

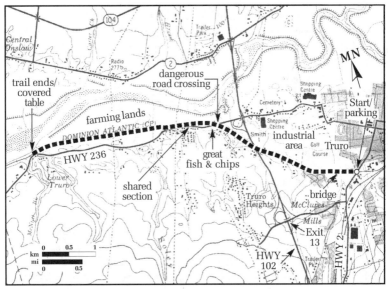

Cobequid Trail

company building on a wide, gravelled surface. For almost one kilometre (.6 mi), it traces the perimeter of the golf course on the right.

At 1.1 km (.7 mi), a sign warns you that you are approaching an industrial area, and, for the next several hundred metres/yards, the path manoeuvres through some busy companies' grounds. At 1.7 km (1 mi), there are benches, compliments of Willcare Paving and Truro Recreation.

Crossing under Highway 102, 300 m/yd later, you will leave buildings behind you for the next 900 m/yd, until you reach Highway 236. The trail crosses the busy road here, and you must be cautious. On the other side is a trailhead, including several interpretive panels. For the next 3.5 km the path will be out in the open, crossing through the farmlands protected by the dikes lining the Salmon River. These are working lands, so remain on the trail.

For the next 900 m/yd, you travel with the road close to your left and farmland on your right. The trail suddenly becomes a paved road, the track having been used to build the road to the new Central Colchester Waste Water Treatment Facility. For 500 m/yd you share the route, and, when road and trail diverge, the path becomes a more natural and grassy treadway.

At 5 km (3 mi), three major power lines cross overhead, and a dirt road, one of many, intersects the trail. Turn left for 100 m/yd and you will find a popular natural spring. Continuing straight, the elevated former rail bed crosses productive agricultural fields, another power line passing overhead at 6 km (3.75 mi). Just 200 m/yd further and the route reaches a small bridge, and begins to curve gently to the left. For the final 300 m/yd you have a great view of the tidal flats, as the road and river converge. You know you have reached the end of the trail because there is a sign that says so! You will also find another covered picnic table. Retrace your route to return to the start.

Cautionary Notes: The trail crosses very busy Highway 236. Extreme caution is advised.

Cellphone Reception: Adequate throughout.

Future Plans: Eventually, the Cobequid Trail will be able to connect Bible Hill, Truro, and the surrounding regions together with a dedicated hiking/biking trail. It may also extend further into the countryside around Old Barns if landowners give permission to use more of the rail bed land.

Devil's Bend

Length: 13 km (8 mi) return
Hiking Time: 4-5 hr
Type of Trail: walking path
Uses: hiking
Facilities: benches, tables,
  outhouses
Gov't Topo Map: Parrsboro 21 H/8
Rating (1-5): 4 [rugged terrain]
Trailhead GPS Reference:
  N 45° 24' 36.3" W 63° 55' 15.6"

Economy River, above Economy Falls. MH

Access Information: From Truro, drive west along Highway 104 to Exit 11 at Glenholme. Turn onto Highway 2 and follow for 34 km (21 mi) to Lower Economy. Turn right onto River Philip Road (dirt) and travel 3 km (2 mi) to the trailhead parking area, on the right.

Introduction: The Kenomee Trail Society has been developing paths in the Cobequid Mountains for several years. In August 2000, the Devil's Bend Trail officially opened, extending far up the Economy River towards the large waterfall.

I think it is fair to say that this trail may not be for everyone, although it is worth whatever effort required to complete. At 13 km (8 mi) for the return trip, this walk is within the range of most fit people. However, hikers should be warned that this is a real wilderness trail. For most of its length it is a narrow footpath. Further, it passes through a rugged landscape of hills and valleys, with the trail climbing the hillside several times. This route is much more challenging than most Nova Scotia hikes, so expect to be quite tired by the time you finish.

Trail Description: The good news is that the first 500 m/yd is downhill, quite rapidly dropping 50 m (164 ft) in elevation. There are stairwells to help you down the steeper sections, and narrow boardwalks cross wet areas. Unfortunately, in the next 300 m/yd you will regain 30 m (98 ft) of

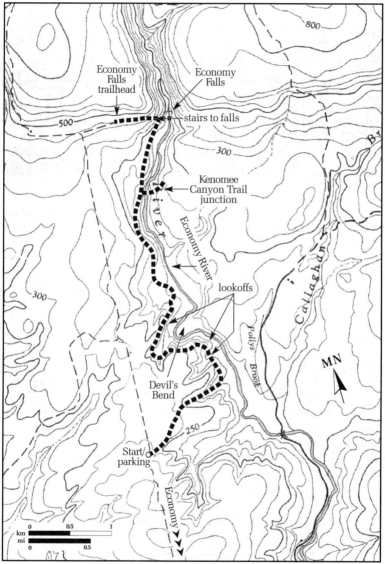

Economy Falls trailhead

Economy Falls

stairs to falls

800

500

300

Kenomee Canyon Trail junction

Economy River

River

Br

Callaghan

lookoffs

Pollys Brook

MN

Devil's Bend

300

250

Start/ parking

Economy

| km | 0 | 0.5 | 1 |
| mi | 0 | 0.5 | |

Devil's Bend

---

the climb, a clue as to what kind of hike it will be. At about 700 m/yd, a woods road crosses the route, and, shortly afterwards, the path descends, paralleling a small stream through a narrow gully. The steep ridges boast gorgeous hemlocks. At 1.3 km (.8 mi), a bridge crosses a tiny brook and continues downhill a further 300 m/yd until it reaches the steep banks of the Economy River.

The trail cuts sharply left, paralleling the river and heading upstream. You walk 10-15 m (33-49 ft) above the water level, and, for the next few hundred metres/yards, the path actually moves away from the river, passing through a lovely intervale bordered by high sandstone rock faces. The trail has actually been designed so that it passes at the foot of these splendid walls. At 2.4 km (1.5 mi), you climb to the first small lookoff above Devil's Bend. From this spot you gain broad views of the Economy River Valley. A jutting elbow of land has forced the river into several 90° turns beneath this vantage point, providing a dramatic vista of river and the wind-and-rain-sculpted 50 m (164 ft) sandstone bluff opposite. Watch the waters in the river below, a common area for deer and bear sightings, while raptors enjoy the convenient perch of the tall trees overlooking this open part of the valley.

The hike becomes more challenging during the next kilometre (.6 mi), climbing and descending as it traces the narrow gorges cutting deeply into the hillside. At 3.3 km (2 mi), you reach the best viewing station yet, perched high above Devil's Bend on the top of a sandstone bluff. Shortly after, the trail intersects a woods road and follows it downhill until you are walking beside the Economy River for the first time, at 3.9 km (2.5 mi). For the remaining 2.5 km (1.5 mi), the trail stays relatively close to the water, although it occasionally moves inland for short stretches. At about 5.5 km (3.5 mi), you may notice a clear-cut through the trees on your left. The river is quite narrow here. With only 400 m/yd remaining, you arrive at another lookoff, although the falls are still hidden by the hills. The trail ends in the middle of the Economy Falls Trail; turn right and descend 105 steps to end your walk at the base of the falls, a 6.5 km (4 mi) walk from the trailhead.

You may return by the same path, but if you want an easier, although much less scenic, return walk, follow the stairs (approximately 180!) at Economy Falls up the hill to the River Philip Road. Turn left, and follow about 4.5 km (2.75 mi) of mostly level walking back to the trailhead.

Cautionary Notes: This is a challenging hike into a remote area of the interior over rugged terrain. Several elementary precautions will make it a more enjoyable and safer experience:

1. Notify someone where you are going and when you will return.
2. Carry a map and compass.
3. Carry a pack with change of clothing.
4. Carry water and food.

Cellphone Reception: For much of the route a cellphone is not able to send or receive calls.

Further Information: An excellent brochure is available at the Cobequid Interpretation Centre in Economy.

Devil's Bend Trail, near Kenomee Canyon Trail junction. MH

Five Islands Provincial Park

Length: 11 km (7 mi) rtn
Hiking Time: 3-4 hr
Type of Trail: walking paths, fields, roads
Uses: hiking, cross-country skiing
Facilities: outhouses, water, campsites, firewood, showers, tables, benches, playground
Gov't Topo Map: Parrsboro 21 H/8
Rating (1-5): 3
Trailhead GPS Reference: N 45° 24' 02.2" W 64° 02' 05.6"

View from Red Head Trail, Five Islands Provincial Park. MH

Access Information: From Truro, drive west along Highway 104 to Glenholme. Turn onto Highway 2 and continue past Lower Economy. Road signs advise of the park entrance on your left. The total distance from Truro is 57 km (35.5 mi). From Parrsboro, drive east 32 km (20 mi) along Highway 2 through the village of Five Islands. Road signs for the park entrance are on your right.

Introduction: Five Islands Provincial Park includes a 90-site campground within its 452 ha (1117 acres) boundaries. Clam digging is a popular activity on the 1.6 km (1 mi) mud flats which are revealed twice daily at low tide, and the beach is popular in the summer.

This is a good walking site for families, with many places to stop and rest. It is very popular in the winter for cross-country skiing.

Trail Description: From Highway 2, drive 1.5 km (1 mi) down the paved access road to the first gate and use the parking lot on the right, where I recommend you begin. Between May and October the campground and gate are open, and the administrative centre is 1.5 km (1 mi) further. The Estuary Trail enters the woods on the west side of the parking lot; a large sign and many red rectangular trail markers fastened to trees mark your route. The path is distinct and wide, although with numerous roots embedded in the trail. Several pleasant bridges bordered by white spruce are found immediately at the start, as the

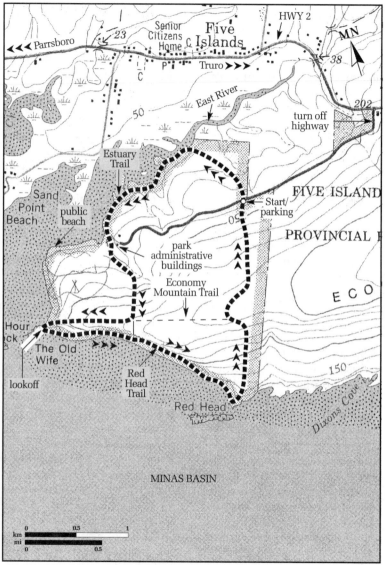

Five Islands Provincial Park

trail begins to curve north and head downhill toward the East River.

At the first junction, stay right and continue downhill. The path widens underneath softwoods surrounded by a carpet of sphagnum moss. Reaching East River, the trees change to mixed hardwoods and the footing becomes wetter. For the next kilometre (.6 mi), you parallel the river, and several lookoffs allow you to view the extensive salt marshes. After 500 m/yd, the trail turns inland to another junction. Continuing straight uphill returns you to the start, so bear right and down the steep hill, around the sharp area cut by narrow gorges. A further 500 m/yd and you emerge onto grassy fields near the administration centre, where you will find washrooms.

The trail enters the woods again below the administration centre at the back of a small grassy field opposite campsites 88 and 89. Look carefully for the tree-obscured ingress. Crossing a power line cut, the path ascends a marvellous ridge 10 m/yd above a brook carving a deep gorge. After nearly a kilometre (.6 mi), you reach a clear-cut planted with pine on your left, continuing until you reach a four-way junction. Turn right, emerging into the camping area through campsite 75, 300 m/yd later. Continue left along the gravel road until it starts to curve, then cut left for 25 m/yd to rendezvous with the Red Head Trail. Turn right and follow the path until the junction with the lookoff side trail, a 300 m/yd branch to the most impressive sight in the park, The Old Wife, a highly sheared, jointed ridge of basalt knifing skyward out of the ocean. Directly beyond are Moose Island and the remainder of the Five Island chain.

Return to the well-signed Red Head Trail, and turn right. For the first kilometre (.6 mi), a steel-link fence parallels the 90 m/yd cliffs. Your path is level and wide, easy walking, with the campground on your left. Reaching a junction after 1.5 km (1 mi), continue straight ahead and gently downhill for another kilometre (.6 m). Watch for lookoffs, some thoughtfully equipped with benches. The remainder of your hike will be more challenging as you approach the deeply eroded slopes around Red Head. The path narrows and descends steeply as it nears this point, and a side trail takes you onto the promontory. The view of the sandstone cliffs over which you walked is magnificent.

After Red Head, the route follows the ridge line, with impressive views and occasional detours into deep gorges, for less than a kilometre before it turns inland for the final climb to the top of Economy Mountain. You face a very steep ascent through mostly dead forest. The bench you find partway up may be a welcome relief. Your final junction is with the Economy Mountain Trail, with a map/sign which indicates that you turn right to get back to the parking lot. You may wish to use the bench here, because there is still some climbing to be done, although mercifully the trail will soon slope downward. Less than 1 km (.6 mi) of continuous downhill remains until you emerge at the gate opposite where you entered the Estuary Trail, completing the grand loop.

Cautionary Notes: Much of the Red Head Trail follows steep, actively eroding cliff edge.

During low tide, large areas of sand are exposed, including a connection to Moose Island. Do not walk there. Tides rise up to 1 m/yd in 20 minutes, stranding the unwary, and the currents produced are irresistible. Access to the Island is only available by boat, which can be locally chartered.

Cellphone Reception: Adequate on the crest of the hill but insufficient reception to complete a call at the trailhead and Estuary Trail.

Further Information: The Department of Natural Resources has a free brochure with a trail map and an outline of services.

Five Islands – Two Different Stories

The five islands at the foot of Economy Mountain, for which the park is named, are prominent in Native legend. Beaver, that energetic but destructive force, ravaged the medicine garden of Glooscap, the powerful Mi'kmaq God-Chief. Infuriated, Glooscap chased after Beaver, hurling five huge rocks at him. The stones all missed, and landed in the Bay of Fundy, where they became the islands we see today.

A different version of the islands' formation suggests they are part of the mostly eroded volcanic basalt cap protecting the underlying stone of the red cliffs. Geologists have found minerals such as chabazite, stilbite, calcite, and agate on them. Rockhounding is a popular attraction all along this coast, where the rapidly changing shoreline reveals new finds every year. Parrsboro contains a geological museum, which offers guided tours. Visitors require a permit to collect rocks, minerals, and fossils in provincial parks.

The Old Wife, Five Islands Provincial Park. Walkers are on the beach exposed at low tide. MH

High Head

Length: 9 km (5.5 mi) return

Hiking time: 3-4 hr

Type of Trail: grassy hill, footpath, old woods track

Uses: hiking, mountain biking, cross-country skiing

Facilities: outhouse, benches

Gov't Topo Map: Oxford 11 E/12

Rating (1-5): 3

Trailhead GPS Reference:
N 45° 36' 42.4" W 63° 33' 40.6"

Access Information: From Truro, follow Highway 104 towards Amherst to Exit 11. Turn left towards Folly Lake, driving 23 km (14.5 mi). Wentworth Ski Hill is on the right with the parking area past the main buildings.

Introduction: For me, one of the great places to hike in Nova Scotia in the fall has to be the ski hill at Wentworth. The woods throughout the valley are almost all deciduous, the view from the hill is spectacular, and the climate is ideal for such a challenging walk: the temperatures are cool and there are no mosquitoes to annoy you on your trek. This walk takes you to one of the best lookoffs in the province, High Head, and it can only be reached by foot.

On a clear day the view can be quite astonishing. Wentworth Valley is spread out beneath you. The brightly-painted houses peek through the trees like out-of-place plants. Trains, using the main line halfway up the hillside across the valley, can be heard approaching for miles, and look like little toys as they pass through. A considerable expanse of the Carboniferous Lowlands – that part of the province on the other side of the Cobequid Mountains – is spread out and visible. Pugwash, Oxford, and maybe even Amherst can be seen through binoculars, and the Northumberland Strait and PEI can be sighted.

The owners of Ski Wentworth are very accommodating to requests to use the trail network. Orienteering meets are often held on the hills' front and back slopes, and Volksmarch clubs also take advantage of the scenic views. Just remember, you are on private property. Take special care to pack out your garbage and leave any equipment left by the staff undisturbed.

Trail Description: The route to High Head is confusing, so pay careful attention to the directions.

From the parking area, take the leftmost route up the hill. As it is one of the ski trails, Robins Run, it is grassy and wide. Within a few hundred metres/yards, you have climbed enough to gain views of the Went-

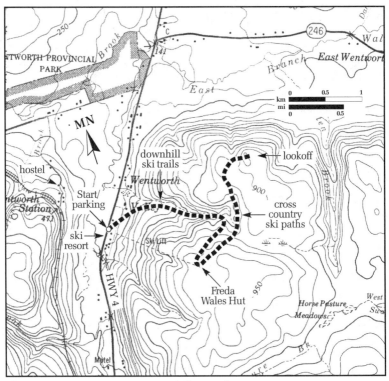

High Head

worth Valley, and at 600 m/yd you reach the first junction, with another run on the right. Continue holding to the left trail as more paths connect on your right. Tiny Henderson Brook bubbles downstream on your left as you climb. At 1.2 km (.75 mi), you reach the base of the Explosion Run. An almost vertical wall will keep you to the left of the trail.

The path somewhat narrows as you ascend the gentler Chickadee Trail. It curves broadly right, widening again to join the start of Explosion near the top of the hill 2.2 km (1.25 mi) from the parking lot. You can see the top of the chair lift to the left; head towards it, and, as you approach, you should notice a sign on the left pointing towards Greg's Pond and a small cabin, the Freda Wales warming hut, where there is an outhouse. The views of Wentworth from the top of the ski hill are magnificent.

Turn off the alpine trails and onto the cross-country ski paths. You will reach a signed junction directing you left 200 m/yds behind the hut. The trees on the hilltop are almost entirely young hardwoods, maples and beech, and wide views are available in the spring and fall. At 3.2 km (2 mi), turn left at the next junction, also signed, and again at the next, 700 m/yd later, where a sign indicates that High Head is left, Scott Trail is right. The route since the Freda Wales hut has been undulating: small inclines and descents, quite enjoyable hiking.

After this junction the path is somewhat rougher walking, but still distinct. Barely 100 m/yd later, turn right at an unsigned junction. Following an old woods road, climb a further 300 m/yd until a sign directs you right onto a narrow footpath. Climbing more steeply through thick softwood, you quite suddenly emerge onto a bare rocky promontory as your reward for the challenging 4.5 km (2.75 mi) hike. One of the widest views available on the Nova Scotia mainland extends before you. A considerable amount of vegetation has been cleared from around the rock, and a cairn has been built to mark the spot.

You may return to the start along the same path, but if you wish to explore you might follow the Scott Trail when you reach the signed junction. This roughly parallels the track you followed in, but is several hundred metres/yards behind the crest of the hill. Many route options are available, but I do not recommend trying these unless you have a good map of the trail system.

When you return to the Freda Wales hut, consider descending the ski hill by another route. After all, from here all trails lead to the bottom!

Cautionary Notes: The complex trail network can be confusing. Carry a compass and set a safety bearing (west) before you start.

Cellphone Reception: Adequate reception throughout.

Further Information:
www.skiwentworth.ca.

Kenomee Canyon

Length: 21 km (13 mi) return
Hiking Time: 6-11 hr
Type of Trail: walking path
Uses: hiking
Facilities: picnic tables,
    garbage cans
Gov't Topo Map: Parrsboro 21 H/8
Rating (1-5): 5 [rugged terrain,
    distance, navigation]
Trailhead GPS Reference:
    N 45° 26' 39.0" W 63° 55' 41.5'''

Overlooking Economy Falls, Kenomee Canyon Trail. MH

Access Information: From Truro, drive west along Highway 104 to Exit 11 at Glenholme. Turn onto Highway 2 and follow it for 34 km (21 mi) to Lower Economy. Turn right onto River Philip Road (dirt) and travel 7 km (4.5 mi) to the Economy Falls Trailhead parking area which is on the right.

Introduction: The Kenomee Trail Society has been developing paths in the Cobequid Mountains for several years. In August 2000, the challenging Devil's Bend Trail opened, and, in 2002, the Kenomee Canyon Trail will permit travel into the Economy Wilderness Protected Area.

This path is probably the most uncompromising wilderness hike in the province. Despite requiring five different stream crossings, including the Economy River below the falls,

no bridges have been built. Signage is limited, and the Department of the Environment insisted that minimal work was performed to improve the treadway. The result is one of the few wilderness standard treks in Nova Scotia and a must for any person who wants an outdoor challenge.

Trail Description: From the parking area, the trail heads towards Economy Falls on the former road, down the stairs towards the foot of the falls, then right on the Devil's Bend Trail for about 1 km (.6 mi). Shortly after crossing a bridge over a small brook, turn left and ford the Economy River. On the far side, the path resumes, a narrow trail climbing the

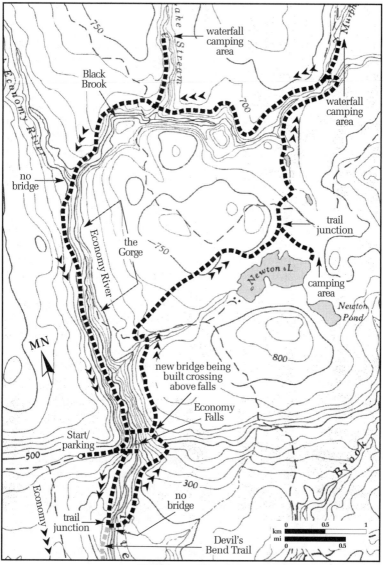

Kenomee Canyon

hillside through thick softwoods. You cross a little brook on a small stone bridge about 800 m/yd later, and at 3 km (2 mi) the trail turns away from the river climbing steeply to follow a gully, turning left on a woods road on the top, about 700 m/yd, and passing through young hardwoods.

Level for only 200 m/yd, the path turns right uphill again on a constructed trail. The route meanders confusingly, twisting and turning around various landforms. The outflow of Newton Lake is quite distinct, however, as you must descend into its steep-sided gully after 5 km (3 mi) of trekking. Once over it, the route turns almost 90° and continues gently uphill though an increasingly boggy and wet area. At 6 km (3.75 mi), an obviously used dirt road cuts across the trail. Continue straight, and follow the path through the densely packed, high ferns for another kilometre (.6 mi) to Newton Lake, visible on your right.

The path skirts the shore of beautiful Newton Lake, and, at about 8 km (5 mi), a sidetrack on the right leads to the first wilderness campsite, 700 m/yd off the main trail. An actively used dirt road cuts across the main trail 900 m/yd later, which follows an older, grass-surfaced road to a small meadow. Look for flagging tape on the far side and stones bridging a wet area. Under softwood cover, the ground a carpet of moss, the path

reaches a small pond, turning left and paralleling its outflow downstream. Almost immediately the land begins to fall away, the slope steepening on both sides. You cross this brook soon, turning right and following a ridge high above another small stream on your left, giving you some of the first views of the hike.

After perhaps 1 km (.6 mi), the path drops down the steep slope to reach Black Brook, which must be forded, at 11 km (7 mi). A few hundred metres/yards along the hillside, a side trail branches right 500 m/yd off the main trail to wilderness campsites next to a small waterfall on Murphy Brook. Downstream, this brook must be forded as it enters Black Brook, and from here the main trail turns left, at brook level, but soon climbing until it reaches the crest of the hill more than 30 m/yd above the stream bed. The path through here is not very distinct, so attention must be paid to your route, and footing is especially rugged at several points.

Chain Lake Stream is reached at 14 km (8.75 mi), and must be forded where it enters Black Brook. On the far bank, a side path follows this small creek upstream for 1 km (.6 mi) to more wilderness campsites located beside a small waterfall. The main trail, however, once across Chain Lake Stream, briefly follows an ATV road uphill. At 50m/yd, the path leaves the road to the right, but shortly cuts perpendicularly across it and once again follows Black Brook on the ridgeline high above. This is a lovely section, especially in the final kilometre (.6 mi) as the path gradually descends to river level. It makes one sudden turn right and climbs above a rocky knoll, then drops to reach the bank of the Economy River just upstream from where Black Brook joins it, almost 16 km (10 mi) from the start.

The final 4 km (2.5 mi) follows the Gorge, the steep-sloped hillside bordering Economy River. Well-signed, it is a combination of a footpath and an old woods road, alternatively climbing and descending, but always with the river audible to your left. Ignore the occasional orange triangular marker; these belong to an older trail, and sometimes the new path has chosen a different route. During the final 500 m/yd descent to the Economy Falls Trail, the roar of the river will warn you of your proximity to this impressive cataract.The trails join at a lookoff above the waterfall with a good view down the river, but you are probably so tired by now that you will turn right and complete the final 700 m/yd back to your car and a chance to rest.

Cautionary Notes: This is a challenging hike into a remote area of the interior over rugged terrain. It is essential to notify someone where you are going and when you will return, and to carry a map and compass.

Bring sandals to wear fording the streams. After storms and during spring run-off, the rivers can be deep and fast-moving. Be extremely careful attempting crossings during these times.

Cellphone Reception: No reception anywhere, except near the trailhead and on the east hillside above the falls.

Further Information: An excellent brochure is available at the Cobequid Interpretation Centre in Economy.

Future Plans: More trails are planned for the Economy Falls Trail System. Wilderness campsites are planned for this trail, with permits available at the Cobequid Interpretation Centre. A bridge above Economy Falls should be finished in 2002.

Economy River, Kenomee Canyon Trail, in late December. MH

Thomas Cove

Length: 7 km (4.5 mi) rtn
Hiking time: 2-3 hr
Type of Trail: former road, walking paths
Uses: hiking, cross-country skiing
Facilities: garbage cans
Gov't Topo Map:
   Bass River 11 E/5
Rating (1-5): 1
Trailhead GPS Reference:
   N 45° 21' 46.0" W 63° 54' 55.7"

Thomas Cove. MH

Access Information: From Truro, drive towards Amherst on Highway 104 to the village of Glenholme. Turn left (south) onto Highway 2. Drive west 33 km (21 mi) to the village of Economy. Turn left onto Economy Point dirt road (signed). Continue until the road ends, following signs, approximately 4 km (2.5 mi).

Introduction: Thomas Cove, near Lower Economy in Colchester County, has trails that are perfect for a hot summer weekend. They are scenic, sufficient distance for most walkers, but designed so shorter walks are available for those overwhelmed by the mid-day sun.

The trail network is organized in two loops, both beginning and ending at the same spot, which is the parking area and beach access. Each of the loops is approximately 3.5 km

(2.25 mi). If you become tired more quickly than expected, you get an opportunity halfway through to stop and rest. There are also some picnic sites near the parking area, and the beach makes a good place to rest as well.

Trail Description: The walk starts at the trailhead in Thomas Cove, on Economy Point. A small parking lot has been cut out almost at the high water mark. The trail's entrance is well-marked, an old road on the right. If the tide is low, however, you can walk from your car directly onto the exposed beach.

The trail follows the old road for only a few minutes before turning off to follow the shoreline, allowing frequent views of the Minas Basin and the Walton Shore across the bay. Sev-

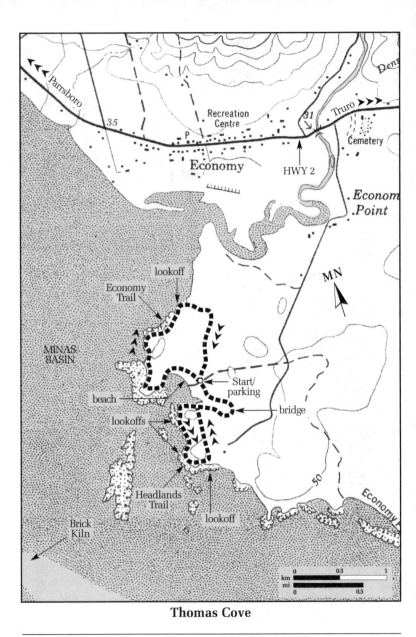

Thomas Cove

eral lookoffs have been created, and log barriers established, wherever the view overlooks a hill or cliff. Economy Mountain and the Five Islands dominate the view to the right, while in the centre of the basin the rocky spire of the "Brick Kiln" (so called on the topo map), or "Brick Hill," stands out even in high tide. During World War II, Brick Hill was used as a target for bomber training.

Roughly halfway through the walk, where the land is curving back towards the mouth of the Economy River, a newly constructed stairway permits access to a rocky beach. From here, you can view either inland or – on a very clear day – sight Cape Blomidon. At low tide, several kilometres of sandy beach extend out from Economy Point. Clam digging is popular, and it is this exposed sand with its abundant life that attracts waves of shorebirds during the fall. The trail follows the shoreline until it reaches

Paddys Cove. The final ocean view is of the beach stretching out towards Economy, with the hills of the Cobequids climbing above the village. The final kilometre (.6 mi) is a narrow, winding trail through a wet spruce bog but this should in no way detract from your experience.

The second loop is the more recent of the two to be finished, and it begins on the left side of the parking area, initially following an old cart track. A small footpath on your left redirects you before the old route ends in the water, but watch closely for it – it is not well marked. This track skirts a deep indentation of tidal overflow, and follows the water's edge inland for several hundred metres/ yards before rounding the water's final advance to return to the headland.

Upon reaching the top of this small bay, you are presented with three options: on your right, a slight descent to a small, sandy beach, on your left,

Low tide, Thomas Cove. MH

a trail inland, and ahead, a path along the water's edge. I recommend following this.

For the next 1.5 km. (1 mi), the trail follows the perimeter of Economy Point as it curves to the left towards Truro. At first you are looking down the Minas Channel, but, as you continue, your view changes to include the shore from Walton and Tennycape to Burntcoat Head. The shores of Economy Point are composed of quite highly erodable rocks. There are several incredible sights along this section, where fragments of the coast have broken away from the rest of Economy Point and are standing alone. Some still have considerable vegetation on them.

After reaching a final viewing platform, from where you can also see cleared fields a little farther along the point, the trail turns sharply into the trees, and quickly returns to the junction near the small beach. From here, you return along the path you entered.

Cautionary Notes: Much of the ocean wall is cliff-face. Although there are fences at all lookoffs, anyone straying from the path might have a nasty surprise. Perhaps a greater risk is from the tides. When low, many kilometres of soil are exposed, and the temptation to venture out on it will be irresistible to many. However, when the tide returns it moves quickly, and it is easy to get stranded.

Cellphone Reception: Adequate throughout

Further Information: The Visitors Centre in Lower Economy has a fantastic brochure available, as well as marvellous interpretative panels detailing the human and natural history of the region.

Thomas Cove, coastline sculpted by Fundy's powerful tides. MH

Ward Falls / Partridge Island

Length: 7 km (4.5 mi) rtn
(Ward Falls)
3.25 km (2 mi) rtn
(Partridge Island)
Hiking Time: 2-3 hr (Ward Falls),
1 hr (Partridge Island)
Type of Trail: walking paths
Uses: hiking
Facilities: outhouses, benches,
garbage cans, picnic tables,
interpretive panels
Gov't Topo Map: Parrsboro 21 H/8
Rating (1-5): 2
Trailhead GPS Reference:
N 45° 25' 24.0" W 64° 25'
28.0" (Ward Falls)
N 45° 22' 13.3" W 64° 19' 59.7"
(Partridge Island)

Partridge Island. MH

Access Information:

Ward Falls: From Parrsboro, drive
west along Highway 209 for 8 km
(5 mi) to Wharton. A green and yellow sign on your right directs you
onto the dirt access road. (If you pass
the sign for the community of Diligent River, you have missed the
turnoff by 100 m/yd). The access
road leads directly to the trailhead,
less than a kilometre away.

Partridge Island: From Parrsboro, follow Main Street – becoming White-
hall Road – towards West Bay for 4 km

(2.5 mi). Turn left at the sign for Ottawa
House. You may park there, or continue to the end of the beach and the
parking lot there.

Introduction:

Ward Falls belongs to lumber and
building supply company C. Ernest
Harrison & Sons Ltd. of Parrsboro. In
memory of founder C. Ernest Harrison, they have taken the land around
the falls out of production and per-
form regular trail maintenance. All
the company's lands are open for re-

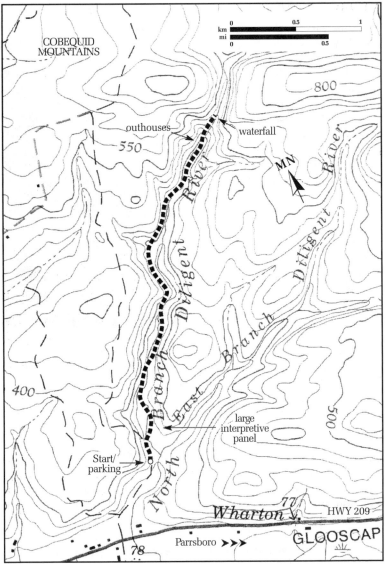

Ward Falls

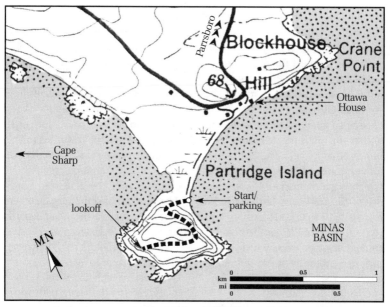

Partridge Island

creational use, and snowmobile clubs have many kilometres of groomed track at other locations.

North Branch Diligent River cuts through the Cobequid Hills, carving a narrow (4 m/yd wide) gorge nearly 40 m/yd long and 20 m/yd deep. In summer, water barely trickles from the opening, and it is possible to climb inside the gorge without getting wet. During the spring, however, the narrow aperture is sometimes insufficient to accommodate the water pressing through, with incredible results. There are few similar sites in Nova Scotia.

You will notice that a long beach connects **Partridge Island** to the mainland. Apparently this was created during the great Saxby Gale of 1869, when gravel blocked the existing channel. Partridge Island also contains a strong magnetic anomaly, strong enough to swing the compass needle of approaching ships. The Island's erosion resistant basalt dominates the entrance to Parrsboro Harbour.

Trail Description:

Ward Falls: A sign in the parking lot, next to a covered garbage can, signals the entrance to the walk. At first an old road, the trail heads up North

Branch Diligent River valley, which is more like a meandering brook, on your right. Within 300 m/yd, the trail separates right off the old road and crosses the brook. There are signs, but these are difficult to spot in the summer. Over the bridge, the route crosses an abandoned field planted with white pine and comes to a large interpretive panel. The trail then moves under a high spruce canopy, which is maintained for the remainder of the trail. The farther up the increasingly steep-sided valley you go, the older and larger the trees become. On quiet days, when a light mist rises from the brook, the moss-covered rocks and old trees look enchanted – or haunted!

As if unable to make up its mind, the path crosses back and forth over the brook on well-constructed bridges, almost too many times to count. In case you lose track, mounted on one of the bridges is a large sign saying "Halfway." Throughout the route are benches and seats carved from tree stumps and there are numerous small interpretive signs. If you walk quietly you may sight a blue heron fishing.

Encountering two large outhouses on your left indicates that you have almost reached the end of the walk. The trail now climbs at a relatively steep angle for a short distance, the sound of the falls growing. A picnic table on your left overlooks the en-trance to the gorge. You will be facing a massive exposed rock wall, rising directly across your path: the Cobequid – Chedabucto Fault. For most, this is where the walk ends. The more adventurous may wish to climb the ladder from the bottom of the falls to the entrance of the gorge, where they will be rewarded with a fascinating view of the cave-like ravine. From there, ropes secured by pitons permit the agile and confident to scramble into the gap, where they may walk a few metres/yards farther until blocked by deeper basins. These pools, though cold, may even invite impromptu skinny-dipping. Whatever your choice, when you are ready, retrace the same path to return, 3.5 km (2.25 mi) away.

Partridge Island: From Ottawa House, walk or drive 700 m/yd to the base of the wooded hill, enjoying the wonderful views in every direction from the exposed barrier beach. A large sign at the trailhead includes a map and a geological interpretation of the area. The trail immediately climbs steeply, a narrow footpath with stairs placed into the hillside. Benches and handrails are available as you struggle to an elevation of 61 m/yd in barely 600 m/yd.

After reaching the crest, the path continues a further 400 m/yd, descending to finish at an elaborate observation centre. This provides impressive views of North Mountain, on the opposite shore of Minas Basin, and West Bay. There are several interpretive panels at the tower, and picnic tables are located in the nearby woods. Retrace the path to return.

Cautionary Notes:

Ward Falls: The gorge entrance is difficult to reach and requires dexterity. Ladder, ropes, and rocks are often slippery from spray. After a rainstorm, or during the spring run-off, do not enter the restricted area of the gorge. Some paths appear to lead above the falls; these are not part of the formal trail system and are not recommended.

Hunting is permitted in this area. Starting in early October, the season varies from year to year and among types of game. Contact the Department of Natural Resources before going into the woods. Wear hunter orange for safety.

Partridge Island: Exercise caution around the steep climbs and dangerous cliffs.

Cellphone Reception:

Ward Falls: Adequate at the trailhead, though none in the valley.

Partridge Island: Adequate throughout.

Partridge Island. MH

Gibralter Hill, Lookoff, Musquodoboit Trailway System. MH

Bridge over Winter Creek, Chapel Gully Trail. MH

Black Duck Cove / Chapel Gully

Length: 3.5 km (2 mi) rtn
  (Black Duck Cove)
  4.5 km (2.75 mi) rtn
  (Chapel Gully)
Hiking Time: 1-2 hr
Type of Trail: boardwalk,
  gravelled walking trail,
  natural surface
Uses: hiking
Facilities: change houses,
  washrooms, tables, canteen
Gov't Topo Map:
  Chedabucto Bay 11 F/6
Rating (1-5): 1
Trailhead GPS Reference:
  N 45° 16' 35.0" W 61° 01' 52.9"
  (Black Duck Cove)
  N 45° 19' 52.5" W 60° 59' 02.9"
  (Chapel Gully)

Access Information:

Black Duck Cove: Driving towards Canso, follow Highway 16 for 71 km (44.5 mi). Turn right on the unnumbered, paved road towards Little Dover. Drive until you run out of pavement, about 7 km (4.5 mi), and then another 700 m/yd on the dirt road. Signs will indicate that the park is ahead on your left.

Chapel Gully: From the junction with Highway 104, follow Highway 16 for 87 km (54.5 mi) to Canso. Turn right onto Union Street and follow it 1.5 km (1 mi) past the hospital to the Wilmot Subdivision. Turn right and the parking area is at the top of the hill, 300 m/yd.

Introduction:

Black Duck Cove: This is a walk for the entire family, particularly if you are looking for a place to have a picnic. In addition to picnic tables on the beach, others can be found along the Coastal Trail. Several of them are cleverly tucked into spaces among the krummholz, the thick white spruce of the headlands, and provide some shelter from the wind. Be sure to sign the guest book at the trailhead in the main parking lot. Another delightful component of the trek is the placement of bird feeders at several places along the trail, with an invitation to bring your own seed. They seem more like squirrel feeders, but watching them can be just as fun.

Chapel Gully: The first project of the Eastern Tip Trails Association, the Chapel Gully Trail permits you to hike to one of the easternmost points of mainland North America. Named for the Star of the Sea Church, which stands nearby, this trail offers rugged ocean coastline, tidal flats, boreal forest, and a burned-out area that is

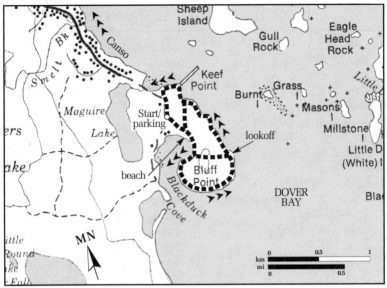

Black Duck Cove

replenishing itself with jack pine, the province's rarest native pine tree. It is designed as three loops, so walkers may choose the most comfortable length for themselves: 1.5 km (1 mi), 4 km (2.5 mi), or 5.5 km (3.5 mi). The path also connects the community to the site of the former "Pest House," a segre-gation compound to house immigrants with communicable diseases during the early 1800s. This trail is a bit more difficult than Black Duck Cove.

Trail Description:

Black Duck Cove: This trail, which opened in 1996, includes an exten-

sive boardwalk component in addition to a well-marked and prepared walking path network. Throughout the length of the hike, two may comfortably walk side-by-side, so conversation can continue even in the face of often fierce winds. The path traces the perimeter of Bluff Point, the small finger of land separating Black Duck Cove from Dover Bay. Fishing boats are continuously heading into or out of Little Dover, and, if you watch closely, you may even be able to sight ocean freight traffic shaving the coast on their way to ports north and south.

From the parking area, the path traces the east edge of the cove, moves around Bluff Point and Flat Rocks,

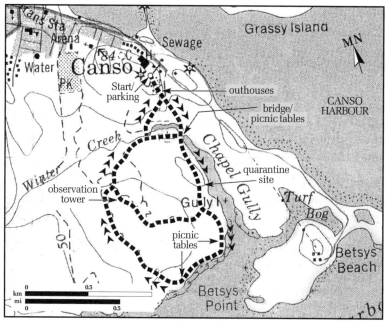

Chapel Gully

and continues to the breakwater at Keef Point. The path then heads almost to the road, then turns into the trees to finish the final 100 m/yd to the parking area. Two connecting paths, one near the lookoff, the other before Keef Point, permit you to shorten your walk.

Chapel Gully: The path descends towards Chapel Gully, a narrow arm of the Atlantic. You reach an impressive 46 m (150 ft) bridge after 500 m/yd, passing tables, drinking water, outhouses, boardwalks, and numerous signs encouraging physical fitness.

Keep straight at the junction in the field, 130 m/yd from the start. Turn left at the junction on the far side, and follow the gravelled treadway uphill. Near the top of the hill the gravel ends, and, 500 m/yd from the bridge, you reach the former quarantine site, which has an interpretive panel.

At the junction 100 m/yd later, keep left towards French Cove, passing several picnic tables, benches, and crossing boardwalks as you trace the coastline. At 2.5 km (1.5 mi), the path turns inland and climbs through thick forest including many jack pine, reaching the observation tower at 3.5 km

(2.25 mi). Climb up and gain a view of Glasgow Harbour and back towards the community. The middle loop also reconnects here.

The final kilometre (.6 mi) features long boardwalks through extensive stands of pure jack pine, and the treadway becomes gravelled again shortly before reaching a junction near Winter Creek. Turn right and reach the long bridge at Chapel Gully, 200 m/yd. Turn left and climb the hill back to the parking area, 400 m/yd further.

Cautionary Notes: During storms, breaking waves and high winds can transform these beautiful walks into dangerous places. Be prepared for variable conditions.

Cellphone Reception: Adequate reception on both trails.

Future Plans: Black Duck Cove Trail; suffered almost complete destruction in a hurricane in 1998. A steady rebuild-ing of the boardwalks will continue.

Further Information: Both trails are part of the Marine Drive Nature Tour system. A brochure of Black Duck Cove is available at local tourism information outlets.

Beechville, Lakeside, and Timberlea (BLT) Trail

Length: 19 km (12 mi) rtn
Hiking time: 5-6 hr
Type of Trail: abandoned rail line
Uses: hiking, biking, ATV riding, cross-country skiing
Facilities: none
Gov't Topo Map: Halifax 11 D/12
Rating (1-5): 3
Trailhead GPS Reference:
N 44° 38' 23.9" W 63° 41' 20.5"

Nine Mile River, BLT Trail. MH

Access Information: From the Armdale Rotary in Halifax, drive on St. Margarets Bay Road, Highway 3, for 6.5 km (4 mi) to the streetlights at Lakeside Industrial Park. Turn right onto Lakeside Drive, and drive for 300 m/yd to the trailhead behind the Coca-Cola plant.

Introduction: New trails are springing up all over the province, the majority being developed by community volunteer associations. Perhaps nowhere did that occur more rapidly than on the section of abandoned rail line connecting the communities of Beechville, Lakeside, and Timberlea. Within two years, a group formed, successfully obtained partnership with the municipal government and other partners, and officially opened their trail in October 2001.

Few paths are as heavily used. A summer evening sees hundreds of people walking, jogging, and bicycling the trail, especially near Governor Lake. Trail hours are between 6:00 a.m. and 11:00 p.m. From 11:00 p.m. to 6:00 a.m., the trail is closed to all users to protect adjacent landowner privacy and to prevent loitering or vandalism. Camping is not permitted.

Trail Description: The walk begins on the west side of the road, where bollards restrict vehicle access and stop signs warn trail traffic of the approaching street. The path is wide, level, and covered with a sealed gravel surface. There are no potholes or wet areas; it is better surfaced than most dirt roads. A speed limit sign, 20 kph, informs bicycles and ATVs – and fast runners, I suppose – of the trail's maximum velocity.

Called the Blue Jay Walk, this first

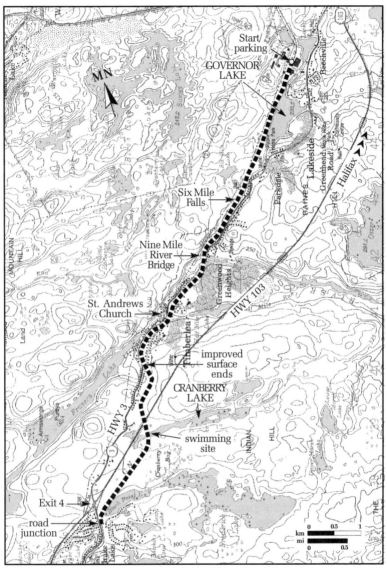

Start/
parking

GOVERNOR
LAKE

MN

Six Mile
Falls

Nine Mile
River
Bridge

St. Andrews
Church

improved
surface
ends

CRANBERRY
LAKE

swimming
site

Exit 4

road
junction

HWY 103

HWY 3

BLT Trail

1.75 km (1 mi) passes through a wooded corridor and follows the shore of Governor Lake to its outflow, Governor Brook. This small lake is quite lovely, and ducks, cormorants, and even loons may be found swimming there. Highway 3 can be seen on its far bank, as can the houses on the lakeside. On your right, the higher ground is entirely wooded, with frequent footpaths leading into the forest.

For the next 2.5 km (1.5 mi), the path is known as the Six Mile Falls section. Governor Brook flows on your left, and there is both an informal crossing and a bridge, about 500 m/yd later, leading into a parking area next to the highway. Six Mile Falls is found on the right a further 500 m/yd, and a small picnic area has been provided. Look for amethyst in the surrounding rocks. Not quite 200 m/yd further, Governor Brook crosses underneath a small bridge, now paralleling the path on the right. The first road crossing is found 100 m/yd later and there are bollards and stop signs posted on the trail.

Highway 3 is now very close to your left and higher than the trail, while Governor Brook is on the right and lower. At 3.5 km (2.25 mi), another street crosses the path, and, at 500 m/yd, you arrive at the larger bridge crossing Nine Mile River. This is another good place to look

around, for there is another attractive pond on the right and the stonework of the road bridge to your left is very interesting.

Once safely across busy Highway 3, you have started the Frasers Mill Walk. For the next 2 km (1.25 mi), the trail passes near many homes and crosses several busy streets, including Brentwood Avenue and Maplewood Drive. The site of the former mill can be seen on your right about 1 km (.6 mi) further by the pond where St. Andrews Anglican Church now stands. After crossing Forest Glen Drive, the trail curves left in a long, sweeping turn. The improved surface ends where a power line and an ATV track cross the trail, approximately 6.3 km (4 mi) from the start.

The remaining 3 km (2 mi) are known as the Cranberry Run, and the trail surface has been graded but not covered in crushed gravel. Walking is slightly more difficult, but still quite easy. Few houses will be seen on this section, although the sound of traffic on nearby roads is a constant companion. Passing through a wooded corridor, the trail gently curves right, then left again, crossing underneath Highway 103, 1 km (.6 mi) beyond the end of the gravelled surface. On the other side of the highway embankment, the view opens somewhat. At 7.5 km (4.75 mi), the trail crosses Cranberry Lake, where there is a wonderful spot on your left to stop for a swim. An ATV track heads into the rocky hills bordering the lake, and might tempt the adventurous to explore. The land here is either bog or exposed rock, and quite sensitive to human intrusion.

Less than 2 km (1.25 mi) remain, the trail passing through thick woods, mostly spruce and larch, to end where Silver Birch Drive crosses the path in Hubley, 9.5 km (6 mi) from the start. To return, retrace your route.

Cautionary Notes: Several very busy streets must be crossed. Extreme caution is advised.

Cellphone Reception: Adequate reception throughout.

Future Plans: A connection is planned to the St. Margarets Bay Rails to Trails and to the Trans Canada Trail.

Further Information: A brochure is available through the Halifax Regional Municipality. Website: www3. ns.sympatico.ca/blt.trail.

Guysborough Nature Trail

Length: 33 km (21 mi) rtn
Hiking time: 9-12 hr
Type of Trail: abandoned railway bed
Uses: hiking, mountain biking, horseback riding, snow-mobiling, ATV riding, cross-country skiing
Facilities: picnic tables, benches, outhouses
Gov't Topo Map:
Guysborough 11 F/5
Rating (1-5): 5 [distance]
Trailhead GPS Reference:
N 45° 23' 21.6" W 61° 29' 58.5"

McAllister Bridge, Guysborough Nature Trail. MH

Access Information: From Exit 37 of Highway 104 at Monastery, follow Highway 16 for 40 km (25 mi) to the village of Guysborough. The office of the Guysborough County Trails Association (GCTA) is at 6 Church Street. Park there.

Introduction: The proposed Guysborough railway extended nearly 100 km (62 mi) from Guysborough to the village of Ferrona Junction near New Glasgow. Between 1929-1931, considerable work was undertaken before the project was cancelled. The rails were never laid and the bridges were not built, even though the concrete abutments – some quite massive – were poured.

The people of Guysborough never forgot their promised rail line, or the prosperity they hoped it would bring. When the concept of the Trans Canada Trail was introduced, they were among the first to see that it could turn their rail line into a transportation corridor of another kind. They have many of the same hopes that the Trans Canada Trail will be an economic stimulus to the village through which it passes, but with, perhaps, more modest expectations.

The Guysborough Rail Trail officially opened the first section of the Trans Canada Trail built in Nova Scotia on June 1 of 1996, and they have not stopped building since. The McAllister Bridge, a 60m (197 ft) cable suspension bridge capable of supporting ATVs and snowmobiles, is a must-see for every hiker.

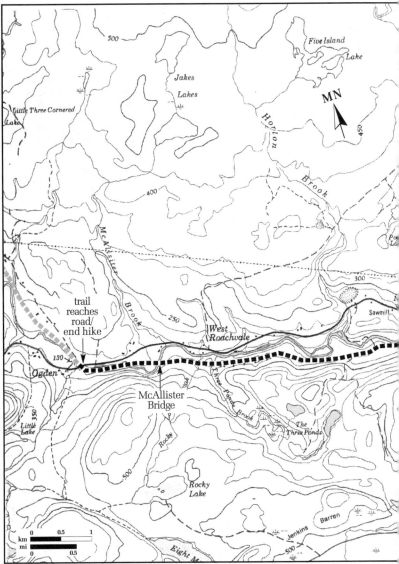

Guysborough Nature Trail (Part 1)

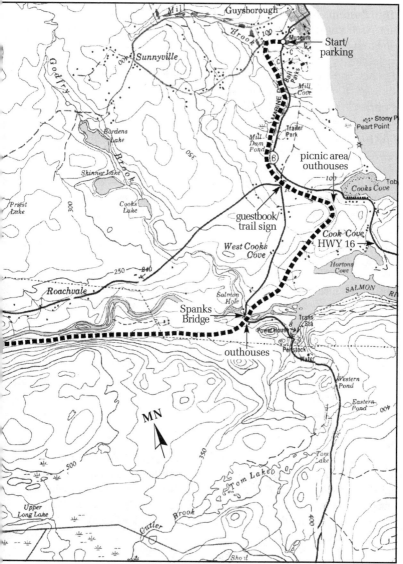

Guysborough Nature Trail (Part 2)

Trail Description: From the parking area, walk one block to Queen Street and turn left. The path begins on the right side of the road opposite the fire hall and an old caboose. It runs through the community, crossing Prince Street and New Road, then heads towards the Mill Dam Pond and the former sawmill. The route roughly parallels Highway 16 until it crosses Route 401 to Larrys River, approximately 3 km (2 mi) from the start. You will pass several interpretive panels, a 50 kph speed limit sign, a small stone bridge crossing Mill Brook, and an outhouse all in the first 2 km (1.25 mi). At the 401, there is a major trailhead panel and a guest book just waiting for your signature.

The trail curves back towards the coastline, providing attractive views of Chedabucto Bay as it rounds the hill above West Cooks Cove at 4 km (2.5 mi). Benches and picnic tables sit on a grassy field overlooking the water, a good place to rest, and there is another interpretive panel and outhouse.

For the next 2.5 km (1.5 mi), the woods are much thicker, providing a good canopy overhead. There is another bench at the edge of fields at 5 km (3 mi), and another outhouse, benches, and picnic tables at 500 m/ yd further. The next kilometre (.6 mi) is mostly a descent through thick white spruce, although the Salmon River is visible at several points. You reach Highway 401 at Spanks Bridge on the Salmon River, about 6.5 km (4 mi) from the trailhead in the village. This is the end of the "front-country" portion of the trail.

Cross the Salmon River on the side, the GCTA has constructed a parking area for trail users, complete with some interpretative signage, explaining that the next section is backcountry trail, with minimal services. From the parking lot, the trail climbs past an outhouse and into the forest. The next few hundred metres are some of the most attractive of the entire Guysborough Trail. The path is an elevated treadway that has completely grown over with white spruce in the 70 years since work was abandoned on the rail line.

All the way to the McAllister Bridge, the trail parallels the ridge of hills making up the Chignecto faultline, which rises on your left, although hidden in the thick vegetation. The Salmon River, on your right and about 10 m/yd lower than the trail, is not visible until more than 2 km (1.25 mi) from the parking area. During this entire section of the trail, you will find no houses and very little evidence of people. For the first 5 km (3 km), you are almost always encased in forest, which seems to swallow all outside sounds and leave you in a tiny perimeter of personal isolation.

At 11.5 km (7.25 mi), the path of the

Maritime Northeast pipeline cuts a dramatic swath directly across the route. Trees have been cleared and the land levelled, with a row of signs precisely positioned in the middle of the clearing. On the far side of the pipeline, you return to the woods, but there is now evidence of logging in the surrounding forest. For the first time, you can see the fields of the farms on the opposite side of the river.

You reach the McAllister Bridge approximately 15 km (9.5 mi) from the start of your walk. Continuing over the bridge, if you can tear yourself away from the foaming river, the path continues 1.5 km (1 mi) to reach the paved road beside the bridge crossing the Salmon River in Ogden. This is barely half the distance of the Nature Trail, but I recommend that you end your walk here. If you planned ahead, you might have a car here to drive back to Guysborough. Otherwise, turn around and retrace you route.

Cautionary Notes: This is a very isolated area; be certain to inform people when you are expecting to return.

Hunting is permitted in woods adjacent to this path.

Cellphone Reception: Adequate throughout.

Future Plans: The route to Cross Roads Country Harbour will be completed and upgraded.

Further Information: A brochure is available from the Guysborough Recreation Department at (902) 533-3508.

Natural Guysborough County

Guysborough County contains seven of the 31 Wilderness Protected Areas in Nova Scotia, covering more than 31,630 ha (78,000 acres) of its land area. When the system plan was developed, it was intended to protect representative examples of all of the different natural landscape types within the province. This turned out not to be possible, because there are so many (77), and some of them are geographically quite small. The province restricted its efforts to only trying to protect crown land. Many of these eco-systems were themselves in privately, not publically, owned land. However, much of Guysborough County is owned by the crown, so several excellent protected places could be designated.

Almost within sight of Black Duck Cove is the Canso Coastal Barrens protected area: 8,501 ha (21,000 acres) of exceptional granite barrens. The barrens contain several species of rare plants, old coastal coniferous forest, distinct fault lines, and an abundance of relatively undisturbed coastal habitats. There is a lot of opportunity for both long distance coastal hiking and canoeing/kayaking around its many islands, coves, and headlands.

Length: 4 km (2.5 mi) rtn (Lundys Firetower)
3.5 km (2.25 mi) rtn (Port Bickerton)
1.5 km (1 mi) rtn (Tor Bay)

Hiking time: 1-2 hr

Type of Trail: dirt road, footpath, boardwalk, rock beaches, sand beaches, ATV tracks

Uses: hiking, ATV riding (Port Bickerton)
hiking, biking, snowmobiling, ATV riding, cross-country skiing (Lundys Firetower)
hiking (Tor Bay)

Facilities: outhouse (Lundys Firetower)
interpretive panels (Port Bickerton)
picnic tables, benches, outhouses, interpretive panels (Tor Bay)

Gov't Topo Map:
Chedabucto Bay 11 F/6 (Lundys Firetower)
Country Harbour 11 F/4 (Port Bickerton)
Larrys River 11 F/3 (Tor Bay)

Rating (1-5): 1

Trailhead GPS Reference:
N 45° 19' 22.2" W 61° 29' 49.0" (Lundys Firetower)
N 45° 09' 31.4" W 61° 42' 08.3" (Port Bickerton)
N 45° 11' 16.1" W 61° 21' 15.1" (Tor Bay)

Port Bickerton Trail. MH

Access Information:

Lundys Firetower: From the junction of Highway 16 near Guysborough with the road to Larrys River, Highway 401, drive 7 km (4.5 mi). Look for a large sign on the left and park on the side of the highway without blocking the road to the firetower.

Port Bickerton: From Sherbrooke, drive north on Highway 7 about 5 km (3 mi) to the junction with Highway 211. Signs advertise the lighthouse. Follow Highway 211 for 25 km (15.5 mi) to a stop sign in the village of Port Bickerton. Turn left, and travel 1 km (.6 mi) on the paved road, continuing straight when Highway 211 goes left. The paved road lasts one more kilo-

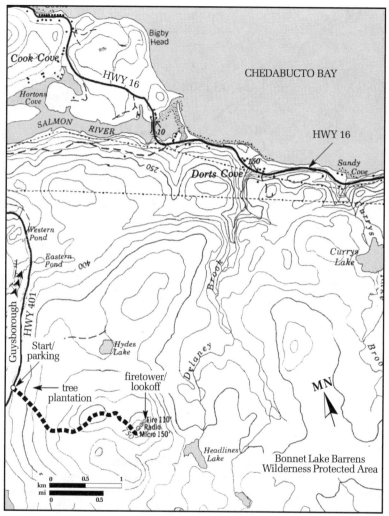

Lundys Firetower

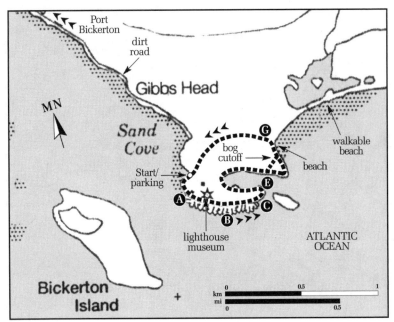

Port Bickerton

metre (.6 mi), then becomes a dirt surface for the remaining 2 km (1.25 mi) to the trailhead.

Tor Bay: Well signed, Tor Bay Provincial Park is 5 km (3 mi) south of Larrys River on Highway 316, then 3 km (2 mi) to the end of the unnumbered paved road.

Introduction: Situated in areas of tremendous scenic beauty, these are all worthwhile visits. The short lengths of each makes them suitable for families as well.

Lundys Firetower: The view from the firetower is almost without equal in Nova Scotia.

Port Bickerton: Port Bickerton was founded in the early 1800s by some fishing families who moved there from Peggys Cove. Originally settling Bickerton Island, most had opted for more sheltered sites on the mainland within a few years. The work on the trails around the lighthouse was completed in 1999.

Tor Bay: Both a provincial park and

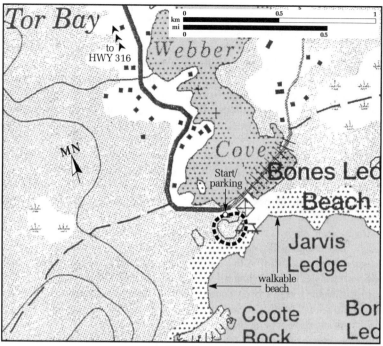

Tor Bay

a provincial historic site, Tor Bay is a delightful place to stretch your legs. Blessed with a wonderful beach, the park grounds were once known as Port Faraday. In 1875, the first direct commercial cable used to transmit messages between Europe and the mainland of North America came ashore here.

Trail Description:

Lundys Firetower: This path is actually the dirt road leading from the highway to the firetower, situated high above the surrounding countryside. The route is straightforward, a 2 km (1.25 mi) walk up the road, climbing most of the time. The view is more interesting and complex. The firetower is situated at the edge of the Bonnet Lake Barrens Wilderness Protected Area, a large, virtually treeless expanse in the centre of the Canso peninsula. It is the highest spot in the county, more than 240 m (800 ft) above sea level, and provides long views in every direction. Isle Madame can be seen north, and the Salmon River valley stretches away in the west.

Expect the weather to be windy and much cooler on the exposed hilltop. Have warm clothing handy, even in summer. There are no trees in the area because weather conditions are often so extreme.

Port Bickerton: At the parking lot, you have a good view of the harbour back towards the village and small Bickerton Island across a narrow strait. Each path junction is labelled with a letter code. You start at A. Right-brain people will probably head immediately toward B. This path works through the thick white spruce by the water's edge, over cobble beach, to a small boathouse 300m/yd from the start. From here, it follows the coastline over a grassy area past the lighthouse and other buildings, across a helicopter-landing pad, and onto the barren and wind-scoured Barrachois Point.

One tiny finger of the trail, from B to C, extends onto a low peninsula reaching toward Europe. Do not walk out here during a storm. There is no shelter, the peninsula is barely 25 m/ yd wide, and it is only 3 m/yd high. Waves easily wash over it.

The path more or less follows the shoreline, turning briefly into the thicker forest in a sheltered low area. This avoids the wettest muds of the marsh, and a boardwalk conveys you across the remainder. At the base of Barrachois Head, Junction E, an ATV trail turns onto a boardwalk across a peat bog. The walking trail continues through the krummholz to the tip of the point, then comes back along the

Lundys Firetower. MH

far side. Low Cape Mocodome is the land visible to the east. Your route continues over the rocky beach, then turns inland at Junction G to return you to the parking area approximately 1 km (.6 mi) away. This inland section skirts the peat bog, and moose and deer tracks are more common than boot prints in this section.

Tor Bay: This is a short loop walk around a barrachois pond and onto an attractive white sandy beach. The path crosses a boardwalk onto a small knoll where covered picnic tables can be found, and continues onto the beach. Although not part of the maintained pathway, several kilometres of walking are available in either direction, so the amount you hike is up to you. Of course, you may just wish to sit back and soak up some sun. The

loop completes itself by crossing a wet area over a long wooden footbridge, and passes through some thick spruce to finish in the parking area.

Cautionary Notes: Hunting is permitted in woods near some of these walks.

All three locations experience extreme weather conditions, especially high winds and lower temperatures.

Cellphone Reception: Adequate reception on Lundys Firetower and Port Bickerton. No reception is available at Tor Bay.

Port Bickerton Lighthouse. MH

Liscomb River

Length: 9.5 km (6 mi) rtn
Hiking Time: 3-4 hr
Type of Trail: former road,
  walking paths
Uses: hiking
Facilities: everything available at
  Liscomb Lodge
Gov't Topo Map:
  Liscomb 11 E/1
Rating (1-5): 3
Trailhead GPS Reference:
  N 45° 00' 41.4" W 62° 05' 44.1"

The fish ladder on the Liscomb River. MH

Access Information: From Halifax, drive on Highway 7 about 111 km (70 mi) to Sheet Harbour. Liscomb Lodge, near the town of Liscomb Mills, is a further 54 km (34 mi) east on Highway 7. The trailhead is found at the roadside after the bridge crossing Liscomb River.

Introduction: The Liscomb River Trail begins at a fairly large and well-marked parking lot on Highway 7 on the opposite side of the Liscomb River from the lodge. There is a large interpretive sign that provides an excellent overview of the hike. Although much of this trail, I suspect, is nothing more than the path of generations of eager salmon fishers following the banks of this well-known stream, the lodge has recently made a great effort to improve the signage and has made the route much more accessible to walkers.

In addition to the featured trek, there are a number of other, shorter walks available. The most enjoyable of these is the Mayflower Trail, which starts in the same parking area as the river path. Mayflower heads to the mouth of the Liscomb River opposite Rileys Island, then traces the riverbank on the opposite bank from the Lodge. Including this surprisingly challenging walk will add almost 2.5 km (1.5 mi) to your hike.

Trail Description: The Liscomb River Trail actually starts on the opposite side of the road from the parking lot,

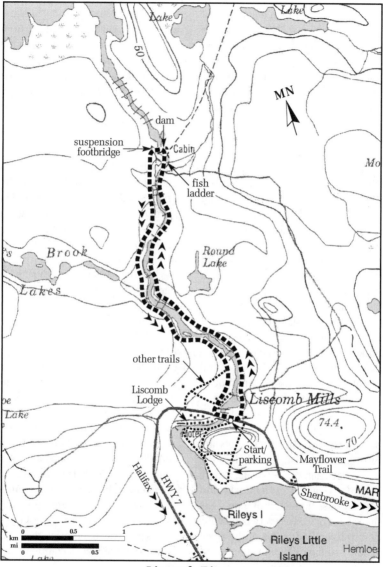

Liscomb River

about 100 m/yd down a gravel road past a lone house. The entrance is unmistakeable: a large gate has been built where the walking route separates from the road, and a footpath meanders through the woods a short distance until it reaches the banks of the Liscomb River.

Signage is excellent, if varied. You may see red flashes or yellow rectangles or orange diamonds (sometimes with arrows underneath), but there is never any mistake about your path, which in any case is well-defined and essentially follows the river.

The footing is somewhat difficult at times. This is a fairly rugged trail, with many rocks and outcroppings, especially between the Watergate Pool and the Grassy Island Pool. The river is often fairly narrow and fast-running. At several places, the rapids are almost mini-waterfalls. But at several points the river widens, and ponds exist where the water is quite slow-moving. Salmon tarry in these pools, taking the opportunity to rest on their trip upstream. Any such spots are well-known to fishers and all of the pools have names: Watergate, Grassy Island, Long Lake, Hemlock, and Powerhouse. In fact, trail map signs have been placed at every pool along the trail, on both sides of the river. They also look like fantastic places to hop in for a refreshing swim on a hot summer day. In fact, they are ir-

resistible – at least to me! There are also many small bridges, ranging from simple logs across the stream to the impressive suspended bridge across the falls at the top of the trail. The woods are mostly spruce, and fairly young, so the viewing is often limited to the river on your left.

The trail crosses Liscomb River at the site of a small dam about 5 km (3 mi) from the start. The footpath reconnects with a gravel road for the final 150 m/yd on the east side of the small concrete barrier spanning the river. In order to permit the salmon access to the waters above the dam, a fish climb of 15 small (.6 m/2 ft) steps has been constructed, and there is an interpretive sign beside it that is quite informative.

The suspension bridge is on the far side of the dam, and traverses a narrow, 10 m/yd deep gorge. This is one of the few bridges of its type in the province, and the hike is worth undertaking for this reason alone. Once on the west side of the river, the path follows the river downstream until reaching a junction with the Crooked Falls Trail. Keep straight, and you soon reach some chalets that are part of the Liscomb Lodge complex. From here, you can either cross the road bridge back to your car, or follow a paved walkway underneath the highway to the main lodge complex.

Cautionary Notes: The cliffs near the

suspension bridge are high and deserve cautious attention.

Footing on the trail can be quite challenging, and it is easy to turn your ankle.

Hunting is permitted in some of the nearby woods. Wear hunter orange during the season, late October to early December, although seasons vary according to species.

Cellphone Reception: Inadequate reception except at the trailhead.

Further Information: Brochures on all the trails may be obtained at Liscomb Lodge.

McNabs Island

Length: 7 km (4.5 mi) rtn
Hiking Time: 2-3 hr
Type of Trail: old cart tracks,
  walking paths, beaches
Uses: hiking, mountain biking,
  cross-country skiing
Facilities: outhouses, benches
Gov't Topo Map: Halifax 11 D/12
Rating (1-5): 2
Trailhead GPS Reference:
  not relevant

Access Information: Regularly scheduled summer boat service is available
from the Cable Wharf in downtown
Halifax. The trip takes about 20 minutes and cost $9.50 plus tax in 2001.
Year-round service can be chartered
from Eastern Passage. Rates and options vary.

Introduction: Few North American
cities are blessed with an island wilderness in sight of their business
and financial centre. The site of a
French fishing station more than a
hundred years before the founding
of Nova Scotia's capital city, and fre-
quented by native peoples long before
that, McNabs has been an important
part of Halifax's recreational area for
generations.

You can reach the island only by
boat, and the ride is enjoyable for its
own sake. Remember, the ocean has

a far different climate, and even the
short distance you travel by boat will
expose you to the winds of the Atlantic Ocean with temperatures 5° or
10° C cooler than on the land. Be prepared.

Trail Description: From the end of
Garrison Pier, turn left along the Old
Military Road. This dirt track runs
the entire length of the island and
was the main artery for supplies between the forts. After 100 m/yd, turn
right onto a small path and walk up a
gentle hill to the site of the former
McNabs Island Teahouse. Once part
of the large Hugonin estate, deserted
since the 1930s, the grounds contain
rare plants such as a massive copper
beech, native to Siberia.

A path north from the teahouse
leads to the Finlay farm site and the
remains of an early 20th-century soda
pop plant. Turn left to return to the
Old Military Road, where you turn
right and head north. The beautiful
mixed-wooded area you pass through
was once the location of picnic
grounds with a large open-air dance
hall, merry-go-round, and carnival
games that drew as many as 4000
revellers playing quoits or cricket.
The trail gently climbs through these
woods for less than a kilometre.

Emerging from the trees, you pass
a number of buildings, some still pri-

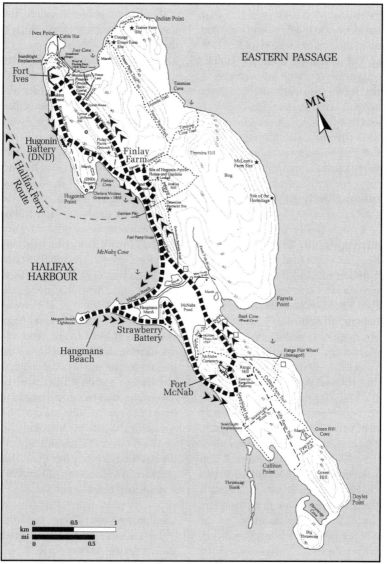

McNabs Island

vately owned. Ives Cove and Eastern Passage are to the right, and only 200 m/yd remains to the ruins of Fort Ives and the northern tip of the island. Superb views of both the harbour and the city are available from the parapet, and this is a wonderful location to sit and enjoy a snack. An outhouse has been sited near the north end of the fort. Fort Ives, however, has not been maintained for many years, and its masonry and ironwork cannot be trusted. Exercise caution around this site.

Exiting the fort, turn right and stroll downhill. A kilometre (.6 mi) long, Forsythe Street, which becomes Garrison Road at the Hugonin Battery, leads back towards Garrison Pier. The trees here are not very old but are full of birds. McNabs Island is also home to white-tailed deer and even occasional visiting moose. At the Old Military Road, turn right and continue past Garrison Pier to the beautiful sand beach beyond it. At its far end is the island's most distinctive landmark, the lighthouse. You can either follow the waterline or walk up an old road to reach it. The point juts almost a kilometre into Halifax Harbour, where you end beneath the guns of York Redoubt situated on the bluff across the narrows.

This is infamous Hangmans Beach, where the tarred bodies of executed sailors once hung in gibbets as a warning to the crews of Royal Navy ships of the punishment for desertion. Follow a boulder breakwater, which is the south-facing side of the spit, back toward McNabs Pond. You may wish to climb the small hill just west of the pond, through thick alder and beech scrub, to the Strawberry Battery. Its guns and searchlights were part of the harbour's submarine defences during World War II. From here you can continue along the McNabs Pond Trail 800 m/yd to Fort McNab.

An easier approach is to follow the Lighthouse Road until it rejoins the Old Military Road, turn right, and walk for about 1 km (.6 mi). The pond will be on your right and Wreck Cove on your left. About 400 m/yd past the pond, turn right at a four-way intersection to see the bombproof vaults of Fort McNab built right into the hillside. Behind and above are the gun emplacements. The concrete blockhouse on the hilltop was the observation and command post, and from this vantage point are the most spectacular views on the island.

The return to Garrison Pier, and the boat ride home, is less than 2 km (1.25 mi). Descend the hill and follow the road the way you came.

Cautionary Notes: There is no fresh water available on McNabs Island. Carry an adequate supply with you, particularly if accompanied by children.

The fortresses are not structurally maintained. Fences, in particular, have decayed, and serious falls are possible. Exercise extreme caution at these sites.

Cellphone Reception: Adequate throughout.

Future Plans: The Friends of McNabs Island Society (FOMIS) is working to have the island developed as a full-service provincial park. They will be installing outhouses, maintaining trails, and erecting signs.

Further Information: *Discover McNabs Island*, produced by FOMIS, is available at most Halifax bookstores. Webpage: www.chebucto.ns.ca/Environment/FOMIS/fomis.html.

Salmon River

Length: 12 km (7.5 mi) rtn
Hiking Time: 4-5 hr
Type of Trail: walking paths,
 former road
Uses: hiking
Facilities: none
Gov't Topo Map:
 Musquodoboit 11 D/14
Rating (1-5): 4 [rugged terrain]
Trailhead GPS Reference:
 N 44° 45' 33.1" W 63° 23' 47.4"

Access Information: From Dartmouth, drive to Exit 18 on Highway 107. Turn left after 1 km (.6 mi) on Mineville Road onto Highway 7, and turn right after 3 km (2 mi). Crossing the river, turn left off Highway 7 onto Circle Drive. At the next intersection, turn left onto River Drive and follow the dirt road for 3 km (2 mi) to its end by the lake or Camp Victoria.

Introduction: This trail was created not by recreational hikers, but by hunters and fishers following the waters to the interior in search of game. Listed in the first *Hiking Trails of Nova Scotia* 35 years ago, a path has probably been in existence along the Salmon River since shortly after the first European settlers arrived around modern-day Lake Echo. The colonists most likely followed a path created by the Native peoples even before that. It is rough, narrow, and winding, always following the waterway, and is heavily used during hunting and fishing seasons. The land

Woody Lake, Salmon River Trail. MH

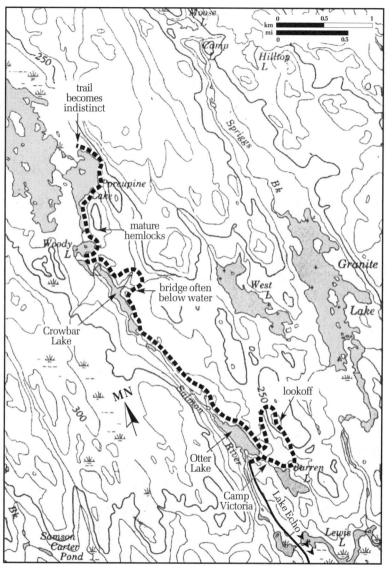

Salmon River

here forms part of the Eastern Shore Granite Ridge Landscape, a prominent feature about 80 km (50 mi) long and 8-10 km (5-6 mi) wide in the interior behind the Atlantic Coast Region. Cliffs which freqently rise sharply to elevations of 100 m (350 ft), large areas of exposed bedrock, and many glacial boulders make for a rugged and forbidding appearance.

This is not a walk for the average family. Unlike the carefully maintained trails in provincial and national parks, Salmon River is simply a beaten path, and I found it easy to wander off the track. But if you want to imagine what it might have been like to wander in the wilderness along an authentic ancient trail, this is the hike you should undertake. It is also a marvellous place to camp, with many excellent spots along the river.

Trail Description: A small sign on the road marks the trail, which crosses the clearing next to the hospital camp. Follow the vegetation boundary left past the camp's lake deck. The path re-enters the woods and descends to a makeshift bridge over a brook. Crossing here puts you on the main trail, but I recommend turning right and heading to the lookoff. Follow the brook and cross a few hundred metres/yards later near Barren Lake. Immediately it begins a steep climb to the lookoff. Yellow and orange flagging tape provides guidance as

you ascend to an exposed granite outcropping with a magnificent view of the river valley, the fire-ravaged slopes on the far side of the ravine, and even the Atlantic Ocean. Note the jack pine around you, an uncommon feature in Nova Scotia. Watch also for bald eagles patrolling the valley; they are becoming more frequent every year and now even over the winter.

Descending on the other side of the ridge, through a second stand of jack pine, complete the 2 km (1.25 mi) loop by joining the main trail just 70 m/yd from the camp. Turn right, and follow the stony path as it skirts the lake and meanders upstream. For the next 5 km (3 mi) you will enjoy the trek alongside this splendid river, although a small brook in the middle of Crowbar Lake may stop you when it is swollen after rains at 2.8 km (1.75 mi). Small Crowbar Lake, Woody Lake, and Porcupine Lake are all lovely, and there is a particularly impressive old-growth hemlock stand between Crowbar and Woody. The trail becomes increasingly difficult to follow between the end of Porcupine Lake and Salmon River Long Lake, and it eventually disappears in a messy bog at the north end of the latter. Advanced navigators and woodsy types may wish to continue upstream, but there is no path. I recommend most hikers turn back at this point.

Cautionary Notes: Hunting is common in these woods. Starting in early October, hunting season varies from year to year and between types of game. Contact the Department of Natural Resources for detailed information before going into the woods. Wear hunter orange for safety.

This is an unsupervised area. Before entering the woods inform someone where you will be and when you are expected back.

Cellphone Reception: Minimal at the start and inadequate throughout most of the hike.

Bald Eagle

Roger Tory Peterson (PMNL, GNL)

As you approach the Salmon River, look closely at the tall spruce trees on the far bank. In the early morning, if there have not been many hikers already, you may sight a bald eagle perched looking for prey.

These massive birds are enormously popular with visitors. In Nova Scotia, numbers have increased rapidly in recent years and at times more than 200 have been sighted simultaneously.

With a wingspan reaching 2-2.5 m (7-8 ft), and its distinctive white head, this majestic bird is unmistakable in flight, slowly riding the air currents with as little wing movement as possible. Once killed indiscriminately as pests, it is now illegal to kill or injure an eagle in Nova Scotia.

Taylor Head Provincial Park

Length: 18 km (11.25 mi) rtn
Hiking Time: 6-7 hr
Type of Trail: walking paths,
    beaches, former road
Uses: hiking
Facilities: outhouses, water,
    picnic tables, change houses,
    interpretive kiosk
Gov't Topo Map: Tangier 11 D/15
Rating (1-5): 4 [distance]
Trailhead GPS Reference:
    N 44° 48' 27.0" W 62° 33'
    42.5." (Parking area)
    N44° 50' 40.4" W 62° 34' 53.3"
    (Gate of Park Entrance)

Access Information: The park is 100 km (62.5 mi) from Halifax on Highway 7, and 11 km (7 mi) before you reach the town of Sheet Harbour. A large road sign marks the entrance; turn onto a dirt road and drive 5 km (3 mi) to the parking lot. Most hikers should continue to the final (4th) parking area; wheelchair access to the beach is available from the first lot. During the off-season, a gate blocks the entrance. Bull Beach is 700 m/yd from the entrance down the road on the left. Watch for the sign.

Introduction: This is a wonderful spot to hike for several reasons. With more than 18 km (11.25 mi) of walking possible, avid trekkers should be able to enjoy a challenging excursion. Because of the layout of the trails, radiating out from a central starting point, several shorter distances are possible for the less ambitious. Finally, the place is simply gorgeous!

Situated on the rugged eastern shore, Taylor Head is a rocky finger projecting 6.5 km (4 mi) into the Atlantic Ocean. Encompassing more than 16 km (10 mi) of coastline, including more than 1 km (.6 mi) of magnificent white-sand beach, the headland is littered with glacial erratics deposited throughout the peninsula.

Taylor Head was granted to Loyalists fleeing the American Revolution. The poor soil was insufficient to support the arrivals. Consequently, like most Nova Scotia settlements, they depended upon a mixture of fishing, farming, and lumbering to survive. A cemetery near the trailhead contains the graves of members of some of the original families.

Trail Description: Three hikes are possible in the park, all starting from the 4th parking area, and each heading in different directions. To complete everything, hikers must return to the starting area after finishing each walk. Since this is adjacent to the beach and the picnic area, ample opportunity is available on a sunny

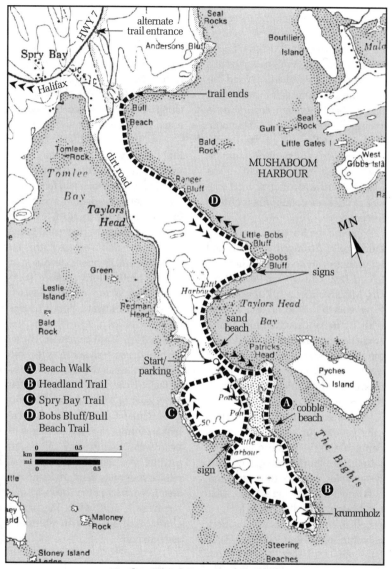

A Beach Walk
B Headland Trail
C Spry Bay Trail
D Bobs Bluff/Bull Beach Trail

Taylor Head Provincial Park

summer day to shuck the pack and relax.

The shortest trail is the Beach Walk. A 2 km (1.25 mi) trip, it begins on the sand at Psyche Cove and follows the coastline as it heads onto a barrier beach system separating a sheltered pond from Mushaboom Harbour. At the end of the beach, either retrace your steps or return on the Spry Bay Trail. This easy walk is ideal for bird watching; several species of duck are commonly found on the pond.

Next are the Spry Bay and Headland trails. Arranged in a stacked loop, these can be hiked either as a 3.5 km (2.25 mi) or 7 km (4.5 mi) circle. My favourite walk, Headland, takes you to the tip of Taylor Head with its rocky coastline and windswept barrens. I recommend following the eastern boundary, crossing the remnants of the abandoned fields cleared by the settlers and hugging the inside of the pond.

After 1 km (.6 mi), a junction permits you to cut across the narrow peninsula to the western coast and follow the shorter Spry Bay loop. Frequent lookoffs face the ocean, and, although rough walking at times, stairs and bridges make it possible for most people to complete this trail comfortably. Turning left and following Headland adds 3.5 km (2.25 mi) to your walk, but is well worth the effort. The trail hugs the rocky shoreline, protected by the stunted coastal forest. Reaching the headland, the krummholz gives way to barrens. Only stunted spruce, juniper, and lichens resist the high winds and fog. The trail almost disappears on the rocky, cobble beaches along the western shore. Rugged and rough, this is a wonderfully scenic hike.

The final trails, Bobs Bluff and Bull Beach, will give you the longest walk in the park, almost 9.5 km (6 mi). Turn left on the beach and follow it to its northern end where a sign and map indicate the start of the path. Narrow and windy, rising and falling as it hugs the uneven coast, this is a hiker's dream. Frequent viewing spots on high bluffs afford vistas of Taylor Head Bay. Watch out for seals at Bobs Bluff; I always notice at least one.

The 3 km (2 mi) path to Bull Beach follows the eastern shore as it gently curves to the slender neck at the base of Taylor Head. You will enjoy splendid views of Mushaboom Harbour and an inland lookoff faces an excellent example of a raised bog with peaty soil. Reaching tiny (but beautiful) Bull Beach and the end of the trail, retrace your route to return to the start area. You are less than 700 m/yd from Highway 7, and, when the park is closed, Bull Beach is an alternative starting point.

Cautionary Notes: Taylor Head experiences high winds and extreme conditions much of the year. Headland Trail hikers should always expect lower temperatures, and should avoid the ocean's edge in stormy and high water conditions.

Cellphone Reception: Adequate throughout.

Further Information: The Department of Natural Resources, Parks and Recreation Division, prints an informative park brochure.

White Lake Wilderness Trail

Length: 17 km (10.5 mi) rtn
Hiking time: 7-9 hr
Type of Trail: abandoned railway
  bed, walking paths
Uses: hiking
Facilities: outhouses, benches,
  covered picnic tables
Gov't Topo Maps:
  Musquodoboit 11 D/14
Rating (1-5): 5 [rugged terrain]
Trailhead GPS Reference:
  N 44° 47' 28.2" W 63° 08' 58.7"

Access Information: From Dartmouth,
drive east along Highway 107 which
becomes Highway 7, to Musquodoboit
Harbour, approximately 40 km (25 mi).
Turn left on Highway 357 for 200 m/
yd. Turn right at the trail sign. A large
parking lot is on the left at approximately 50 m/yd.

Introduction: One the most challenging hikes found in this book, the
White Lake Wilderness Trail is designed for those who enjoy a challenge. No compromises have been
made on the route selection; if there
is a hill nearby, you will be climbing
it. Walking along the abandoned rail
line to the end of Bayer Lake and re-

Eunice Lake Lookoff, White Lake Wilderness Trail. MH

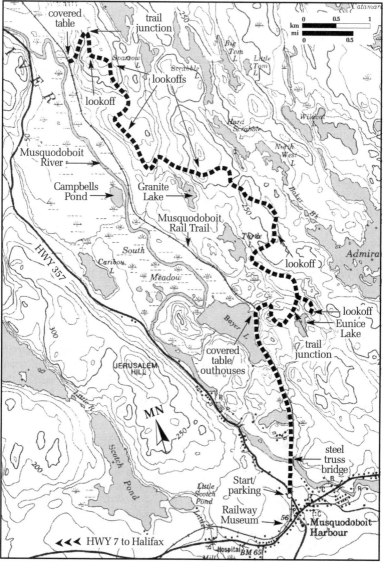

White Lake Wilderness Trail

turning permits a pleasant 5 km (3 mi) saunter suitable for any fitness level. Turning onto the wilderness loop is only for the fit. Wear sturdy footwear for this one, and carry lots of water. Do not forget either binoculars or camera and expect sore muscles afterward.

A volunteer association created this wonderful trail network. Their first project was the 14.5 km (9 mi) rail trail that is part of the Trans Canada Trail. In 2000, they opened the 9 km (5.5 mi) Admiral Lake Loop. The White Lake Wilderness Trail is the first section of a 20 km (12.5 mi) wilderness hiking trail that will travel into the 4558 ha (11,262 a) White Lake Wilderness Protected Area – one of 31 such sites designated by the province in 1998.

Trail Description: You will first be following the abandoned rail line, crossing the Musquodoboit River a few hundred metres/yards from the start on the redecked steel truss bridge. At 1 km (.6 mi), you will find a signpost and the first of many benches. About 600 m/yd further on, a woods road intersects the trail on the right, and you will soon sight Bayer Lake. The trail is now squeezed between Bayer Lake and a massive granite rock face on the right. Several benches face the lake, and, at 2.3 km (1.5 mi), a covered picnic table, bench, and bicycle rack sit beside a slender sandy beach. Perhaps 100 m/yd fur-

ther on the right is a new outhouse, and beyond that the first reconstructed bridge on the rail line.

Between the outhouse and the bridge, next to an old concrete foundation, a narrow footpath leaves the rail bed and begins to climb the steep hillside. This footpath is rugged, rocky, and covered in moss and lichen. Ascending the reverse slope of the hillside the trail will take you to a magnificent viewing platform, signed "Jessie's Diner" on the bare granite summit. You can see far up and down the Musquodoboit River Valley, and easily spot the covered table on the rail line 45 m (150 ft) below.

Immediately the trail descends through dense conifers until it reaches a tiny brook 300 m/yd from Jessies Diner. Cutting sharply left, you climb again, glimpsing Eunice Lake through the branches to your right. The route is never level, moving up and down innumerable knolls and skirting the many granite boulders carelessly littered by glaciers. About 3.5 km (2.25 mi) from the start of the hike, you reach a junction with wooden signs pointing left for the Wilderness Trail.

All the main junctions are extremely well signed, and the route is marked with flagging tape. Even so, it is difficult to follow at several points. For the next 6.5 km (4 mi), you will be following a linear footpath, with half-a-dozen serious climbs. Views are wonderful, but it is truly rugged hiking through rocky terrain. Just 300 m/yd after the junction, a side trail leads right to a lookoff above small Eunice Lake. The view is well worth the short diversion and climb. Back on the main path, which alternately descents and climbs, Turtle Lake is visible to the left about 1 km (.6 mi) later. There is a tremendous lookoff facing Admiral Lake at the 5 km (3 mi) point at the top of a long climb. This is a location well worth spending some time at, viewing the surrounding countryside.

The trail beyond is truly too winding and varied to describe adequately. Massive rock walls, thick vegetation, punishing climbs, and lookoffs above Granite Lake, the Musquodoboit River, Campbells Pond, and Sparrow Lake, fill the next 4 km (2.5 mi). There is even a small stream to be forded near the north end of Granite Lake. The most navigationally difficult location occurs after about 9 km (5.5 mi) at the lookoff viewing Sparrow Lake, to the east. The path, on bare rock, turns 90°left and crosses the top of the hillside. There are few trail markings, and you may need to search for where the path re-enters the forest near the northeast base of the large exposed granite hilltop.

From here you enter some of the most attractive woods of the walk. The path moves along a steep east-sloping hillside, and mature hemlocks dominate. When you reach the next junction, turn left, and follow the slender footpath down the rugged hillside. Under the thick evergreen canopy, a flooring of brilliant green moss covers everything but your route. You emerge at the covered picnic table at the half-way point of the rail trail, after a punishing 10 km (6 mi). Turn left, and follow the gentle, level walkway 7 km (4.5 mi) to return to the trail-head.

Cautionary Notes: This path is extremely rough, and it is easy to twist an ankle. You are quite isolated, so familiarity with map and compass is essential.

Cellphone Reception: Adequate throughout.

Future Plans: This trail will be completed as far as Gibraltar Rock in 2002 or 2003, connecting with the end of the rail trail.

Further Information: There is a brochure available at the local tourist bureau. Website: http://home.istar.ca/~rainbow/Index.htm.

Beach above Scotch Point, Thomas Raddall Provincial Park. MH

Sandy treadway, Green Bay – Broad Cove Trail. MH

Aspotogan Rail Trail

Length: 23 km (14.5 mi) rtn
Hiking Time: 5-7 hr
Type of Trail: abandoned rail line
Uses: hiking, biking, horseback
    riding, snowmobiling, ATV
    riding, cross-country skiing,
    dog sledding
Facilities: picnic tables
Gov't Topo Map:
    LaHave Island 20 A/1
Rating (1-5): 4 [distance]
Trailhead GPS Reference:
    N 44° 38' 08.7" W 64° 04' 20.4"

Access Information: In Hubbards, about 44 km (27.5 mi) west of Halifax, take Exit 6 off Highway 103. The trail starts at the junction of Highway 3 and Highway 329, 1 km (.6 mi) left from the junction with Highway 3. The parking area is on the right.

Introduction: This path follows the abandoned rail line on the South Shore between Hubbards and East River, cutting across the top of the Aspotogan Peninsula. I think bicyclists will most enjoy it. The improved gravel surface is wonderful for them. Families will find this an easy walk because it is nearly level throughout.

Birders should also enjoy this walk. There is a large burn area that is regenerating and it is a wonderful breeding ground for many species.

Naturalists may be eager to observe the rare slender leaf goldenrod, which can be found in a large boggy area right in the middle of the trail. Heritage enthusiasts might take interest in the fact that the trail incorporates the original granite culverts constructed 100 years ago for the railroad. Some of the railroad mile marker signs can also be spotted.

Trail Description: This is a very easy walking experience for people who enjoy woodlands. Although a few houses are visible through the trees at several places, the area is very sparsely settled. After about 1.5 km (1 mi), the wide, gravelled path heads into the interior of the peninsula, no longer paralleling Highway 3 as it did from the start.

At 2 km (1.25 mi), you will encounter a metal post located in the centre of the treadway. This is to warn and slow motorized users before a road crossing. The Half Mile Brook is crossed 700 m/yd later, and you will soon sight Fox Point Lake on your left. Many cottages line its shores, and numerous dirt roads cross the trail for the next 700 m/yd. Beyond the final road, a large metal gate bars access to the trail by trucks. You will note the thick growth of young pine growing on the edge of the treadway.

Noonan Lake comes into view at

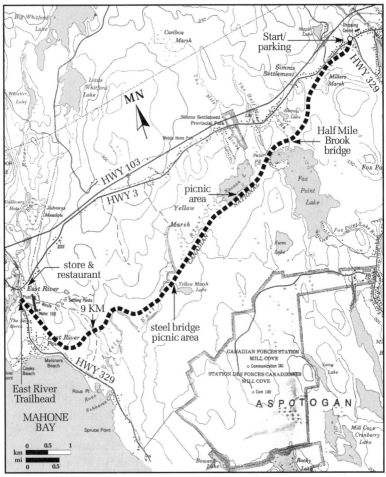

Aspotogan Rail Trail

4.5 km (2.75 mi), and a large new house dominates the opposite side. Once you leave the lake, the scenery settles into forest and bog. Small bridges are crossed at 5.2 km (3.25 mi) and 6.8 km (4.25 mi), and, about 7.5 km into the walk, the trail crosses the Little East River. The railroad constructed a small steel bridge, and the trail association has decked it to improve the footing. The stream, especially in summer and fall, is flowing fairly gently, and it is just deep enough here for a quick, relaxing dip to wash off the sweat from your hike. It is also a wonderful place to sit and eat your lunch.

The path now begins to narrow and pass through more hilly terrain. You sight Little East River again to the left 900 m/yd after the bridge, and it remains visible through the trees for several hundred metres/yards as the path curves gently left. At 9 km (5.5 mi), a former road, now used only by ATVs, crosses the trail. Just 100 m/yd beyond, cattails, growing in a large swamp on the right, crowd into the path.

Houses are visible again during the final 2 km (1.25 mi). You will sight beautiful Mahone Bay on your left after nearly 10 km (6 mi), and Highway 329 is visible only 200 m/yd away across a field. However, the trail curves right, settling into a long straightaway for the final 1.5 km (1 mi). A large factory is prominent along the final kilometre (.6 mi).

The trail, completing an 11.5 km (7.25 mi) tramp, emerges on busy Highway 329 at East River, an alternate start/finish. Turn right for 200 m/yd and you will reach a store and a restaurant at the junction with Highway 3. Retrace your route to return to your car.

Cautionary Notes: Wood ticks are active from April to July.

Many motorized vehicles use this trail, so walkers need be observant and be prepared to step aside.

Hunting is permitted in adjacent woodlands.

Cellphone Reception: Adequate throughout.

Future Plans: This will become part of the Western Loop of Nova Scotia's Trans Canada Trail. Nearby groups working on other sections include St. Margarets Bay Rails to Trails, Hubbards to Hubley, and the Municipality of Chester: East River to Martins River.

Length: 16 km (10 mi) rtn
Hiking Time: 3-5 hr
Type of Trail: abandoned railway bed
Uses: hiking, mountain biking, cross-country skiing, wheelchairs
Facilities: garbage cans, tables, benches
Gov't Topo Map:
Bridgewater 21 A/7
Rating (1-5): 2
Trailhead GPS Reference:
N 44° 21' 49.5" W 65° 10' 58.4"

Access Information: From downtown Bridgewater, follow King Street on the west bank of the LaHave River, approximately 1.6 km (1 mi) from the streetlights at Victoria Road and the road bridge.

Introduction: Shortly before the provincial government acquired the abandoned rail line running between Halifax and Liverpool, the town of Bridgewater purchased the section inside its municipal boundaries. Passing through the centre of town and following alongside the LaHave River, this made for an ideal community trail, and it was not long before construction began.

The centrepiece of the system is the bridge crossing the LaHave, a massive steel structure perched high above the stream. With a great deal of financial support from the Michelin Tire Company, whose familiar logo

LaHave River Bridge, Centennial Trail. ᴍʜ

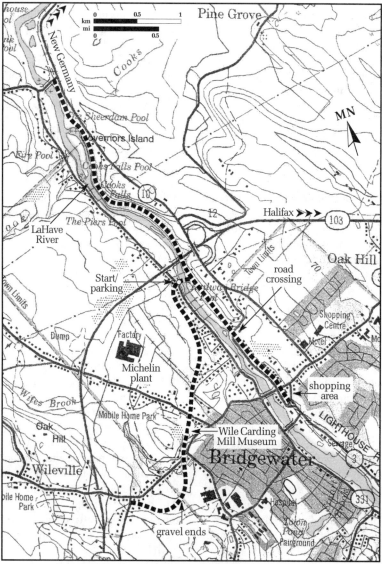

Centennial Trail

now adorns the side of the bridge, it was restored in truly grand style. In addition to the usual decking and railing, covered picnic tables, located near the middle of the span, were part of the integrated development. This makes it a favourite spot for walkers and bikers to rest, and enjoy the view downstream. The Centennial Trail opened on July 31, 1999, and is easy walking, suitable for families.

Trail Description: From the parking lot at the LaHave River Bridge, you have three options: left towards the Wile Carding Mill Museum, right across the bridge and then right to downtown Bridgewater, or right across the bridge and left to Cooks Brook. Climb the stairs from the parking lot below and make your choice.

Option 1: Turning left, the path, a 3 m/yd-wide fully gravelled treadway, heads gently uphill through a cut in the slate rocks of the river's ridgeline. Magnificent white pines crown these hills, and, for 1 km (.6 mi) until shortly before York Street, these woods crowd close to the route. When you begin to see houses, you are within 200 m/yd of the York Street/Starr Street crossing to the entrance of the Bridgewater Industrial Park and a busy road. St. Phillips Street, 300 m/yd beyond York, is also busy. Both places have crosswalks and signage for the trail.

Continuing uphill, the path heads through a thickly brushed area for 400 m/yd until it emerges to cross quiet Pearl Street. From here to Victoria Road, almost 2 km (1.25 mi) into your walk, the rail line is raised above the surrounding land. To your left are the attractive grounds surrounding the Wile Carding Mill Museum, easily accessed from the path. At Victoria Road, caution must be taken to cross this busy highway only where indicated. You will then follow the path to the right, parallel to Victoria Road, for about 100 m/yd until it turns left into the forest, crossing an attractive little bridge by a small pool of water. For the next 500 m/yd, the gravel continues, then, for the final 500 m/yd to William Wile Road, the surface is natural and the vegetation has not been trimmed back. When you reach the road, return and retrace your route to the bridge, a 6 km (3.75 mi) return trip.

Option 2: Turning right on the La-Have River Bridge, cross the structure to arrive at a junction at 200 m/yd. Signs will tell you that turning right will take you to the downtown area. If you choose this option, you will descend through thick forest, the river occasionally visible to your right, to arrive at LaHave Street 700 m/yd later. From here you can follow either the gravelled trail or a sidewalk through a residential area for 1 km

(.6 mi) to Aberdeen Street and a large shopping area including restaurants. Retrace your steps to the intersection at the LaHave River Bridge, having walked 3.5 km (2.25 mi).

Option 3: The other sign at the La-Have River Bridge junction states that Cookville is towards the left. This section is the most remote of the trail, especially once you cross under Highway 103, 300 m/yd beyond the junction. The trail is high above the river, on your left, and many of the pines and hemlocks lining the banks are quite old, providing some shade for the path. At about 1.5 km (1 mi), you will pass under some power lines and reach Cooks Falls. A path permits you to leave the rail line and descend the steep hillside to the cataract below. This is a busy fishing site in season.

The improved surface on the trail ends 300 m/yd beyond Cooks Falls, and there is a Centennial Trail sign there to mark the start of that path. However, you may easily continue another 1.5 km (1 mi) along the clear pathway, paralleling both the river and Highway 10, which you remain close to for the final 1 km (.6 mi). The trail finishes when the rail line intersects the highway 3 km (2 mi) from the LaHave River Bridge. Once again, retrace your path to return to the start.

The total distance of all three sections as described is 16 km (10 mi).

Cautionary Notes: Wood ticks are active from April to July.

Several busy roads must be crossed, so use caution.

Cellphone Reception: Adequate throughout.

Future Plans: Eventually this trail will link with other Lunenburg County trails and then the Trans Canada Trail. In as little as 3 years, it may be possible to hike from Halifax to Bridgewater, more than 100 km.

Further Information: The municipality produces a brochure, available at the local Tourist Bureau.

Gold Mines / Hemlocks and Hardwoods

Length: 3 km (2 mi) rtn
(Gold Mines)
6 km (4 mi) rtn
(Hemlocks and Hardwoods)
Hiking Time: 1-2 hr each
Type of Trail: walking path,
former road
Uses: hiking, cross-country skiing
Facilities: outhouse, garbage can,
picnic table, benches
Gov't Topo Map:
Kejimkujik 21 A/6
Rating (1-5): 1
Trailhead GPS Reference:
N 44° 21' 49.5" W 65° 10' 58.4"
(Gold Mines)
N 44° 26' 32.2" W 65° 15' 11.9"
(Hemlocks and Hardwoods)

Access Information:

Gold Mines: Follow the paved road from the Kejimkujik National Park entrance to the fish hatchery on Grafton Lake, approximately 11 km (7 mi). Follow the gravel road continuation another 3.5 km (2.25 mi). The parking area and trailhead are on your left, and are well signed. The gate may be closed at Grafton Lake in the winter, adding 7 km (4.5 mi).

Hemlocks and Hardwoods: From the park entrance, drive 5 km (3 mi) to the turnoff for Jeremys Bay Camp-

ground. Turn right and follow the road over the Mersey River. On the far side of the bridge, the road divides, with a dirt road going right. Follow this 3 km (2 mi) to a parking lot. The trail starts at its far end.

Introduction:

Gold Mines: Abandoned mine shafts, long narrow trenches from "snake diggin'," and the remains of mining equipment can be found along the self-interpretive trail. This is a pleasant walk accessible to almost any fitness level. Interpretive panels, railings, and benches make this an excellent choice for a short, interesting walk.

Hemlocks and Hardwoods: Very little of the original forest in Kejimkujik survived the logging boom of the 1800s, but isolated groves of old-growth eastern hemlock, some as old as 300 years, can still be found. A significant stand of these graceful softwoods is located near the northern edge of Big Dam Lake. A trail has been created to make these trees accessible to nature lovers, and it offers the most spectacular forest walk in the province. Relatively short and level, this trail is excellent for families and people of most fitness levels.

Trail Description:

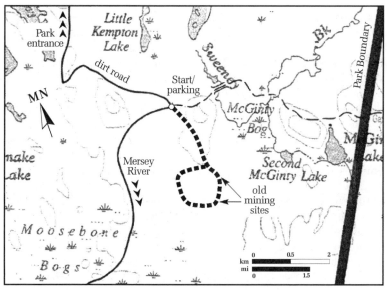

Gold Mines

Gold Mines: Two trails, McGinty Lake and Gold Mines, start from the parking lot. A garbage can, picnic table, and washroom are found by the parking area, but there is no water source anywhere on the trail.

Narrow and winding at first, the gravelled track provides excellent footing. An interpretive panel near the parking lot sets the scene for the story of gold mining in Kejimkujik. A second sign, 100 m/yd later, explains the geographical features of the landscape. The path joins an old road emerging from the left, and a large bench is positioned at this intersection. Turn right, and follow the gravel track as it leads gradually downhill to another

sign. This panel also talks about geology; note that examples of the quartzite rock it mentions are piled at its base. At the top of a small rise 150 m/yd beyond, an arrow directs traffic left onto a short loop that explores the actual mining site.

In the next 500 m/yd, interpretive panels outline the story of the men who searched for gold on this spot and their methods. The trail circles through the debris of their digging, eventually returning to the old road that was their supply line. I found the last interpretive spot, featuring old equipment, particularly interesting. The loop is completed shortly past this spot, and walkers must retrace their path to return to the parking lot.

Hemlocks and Hardwoods: This short loop begins at the Big Dam parking lot, which is also the trailhead for the Channel Lake Trail and the Liberty Lake Loop Trail as well as a popular starting point for canoe trips. The initial kilometre (.6 mi) features quite a few side trails and path junctions; keep to your right, heading uphill, until you reach the junction with campsite 1, the inland path, and the lakeshore route. I recommend the lakeshore route – this path offers an easy stroll with the lake always in sight on your left – and save the hemlock stand for near the end.

The woods at first feature large-toothed aspen, red maple, red oak, and white birch. After about 2 km (1.25 mi), the trees begin to change, with hardwoods giving way to mixed spruce, hemlock, and pine. Within another kilometre (.6 mi), you will encounter a well-signed junction; turn right and head inland.

The inland trail only goes east for a short distance before it turns another 90° and you cross a lengthy boardwalk over an open, swampy area of cinnamon ferns growing under black spruce. Suddenly you are transported into a completely different world. The low scrubs give way, and the leafy ceiling climbs higher and higher. You are inside a massive arboreal cathedral, the huge trunks of the hemlocks form the columns supporting the dome of the canopy far overhead.

Very little light penetrates here, giving an impression of perpetual twilight. Little can thrive in the thick

Gold Mining

In 1884, Jim McQuire, hiding in the woods to evade the law, discovered gold 9 km (5.5 mi) east of this spot. Gold fever soon spread, and mines were opened throughout south central Nova Scotia. A Caledonia businessman, Nelson Douglas, was the first to work this area, claiming the land from 1888 to 1890. He soon sold his interests to Charles Ford, a Maitland Bridge lumberman, whose family went on to work this claim for 30 years, even though very little gold was found.

In 1922, John McClare, a former prospector who had worked for Nelson Douglas, found a 6 cm (2.5 in) vein of gold in the quartzite rock. Named "Blue Lead," this thin vein was not large enough to be profitable, but it was too enticing to abandon. McClare died in 1932, never having found the mother lode he expected. His son Horace continued to work the claim until 1939. Heavy rains that spring flooded the most promising sites and the outbreak of World War II finally forced an end to the exploration. The claims lapsed, and the "big gold," if present, is still undiscovered.

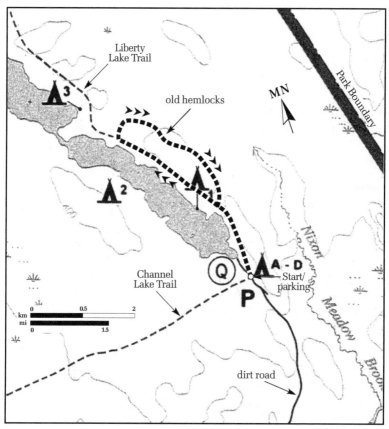

Hemlocks and Hardwoods

carpet of decaying hemlock needles, so no other plants cover the forest floor. Only where one of the trees has fallen, admitting a shaft of light, does new growth appear. These are some of the few remnants of the Acadian forest that many believe covered the New World of the original European explorers. I am always humbled in the presence of these magnificent giants. This is, without a doubt, a very special place.

Once past the hemlock stand you are just over halfway into the hike, although to some the remainder may seem anticlimactic. You still pass through some attractive forest, as the trees change back to hardwoods. When you encounter the next junction, turn left, and, in less than a kilometre (.6 mi), you are back to the Big Dam parking lot.

Cautionary Notes: Wood ticks are active from April to July.

The hemlock ridge is a Special Protected Area in the park. Be particularly careful not to cause damage.

Cellphone Reception: Adequate reception on both trails.

Further Information: An interpretive brochure called *The Forests*, available at the Information Centre at the park entrance, is particularly useful when walking the Hemlock Trail. A page with a map and brief description of all day walks accessible in the park is also available.

Green Bay – Broad Cove

Length: 12 km. (7.5 mi) rtn
Hiking time: 3-4 hr
Type of Trail: old cart track, dirt road
Uses: hiking, mountain biking, horseback riding, cross-country skiing
Facilities: stores at either end
Gov't Topo Map:
LaHave Island 20 A/1
Rating (1-5): 3
Trailhead GPS Reference:
N 44° 12' 17.6" W 64° 26' 21.7"

Access Information: From Halifax, take Highway 103 past Bridgewater to Exit 15 at Italy Cross, about 115 km (72 mi). This is also the turnoff to Rissers Beach Provincial Park. Turning left for 11 km (7 mi) will take you to Petite Riviere and Highway 331. The road to Green Bay starts by the southside of the one-lane bridge in Petite Riviere, 3 km (2 mi) of paved road.

About 500 m/yd before the pavement ends is a small public beach and a store: MacLeod's Canteen. You might choose to park here and wander through the lovely resort community of Green Bay. The road is very narrow and there is not very much traffic. Otherwise continue to the end of the pavement, near a sandy area by Long Point, where parking is available.

Introduction: If you like ocean, waves, sandy beaches, and seabirds, you will love this walk. An old cart track follows the coastline for its entire length, although it is no longer maintained by the Department of Highways. This is a lovely coastal hike between the villages of Green Bay and Broad Cove that can be either a family walk or an enjoyable hike. The trail is wide and mostly level with only one or two difficult spots.

Every little cove has its family of eider ducks, that travel in groups of several females and their chicks. They are very shy, and will head out to sea as soon as they detect your approach. If you have binoculars, scan the waters not far offshore. A little investigation will probably reveal large rafts of eiders, often hidden by the swell, with their numbers only revealed to patient watchers.

Trail Description: If you parked at MacLeod's, the first few hundred metres/yards will follow pavement, passing the cottages of summer residents. If it is a sunny day, expect plenty of company. This is a very pretty spot, and the beach is a good place to leave anyone not keen on hiking. The paved road continues as far as the sandy barrachois at Long Point, the track threading between ocean and freshwater. Few cars can

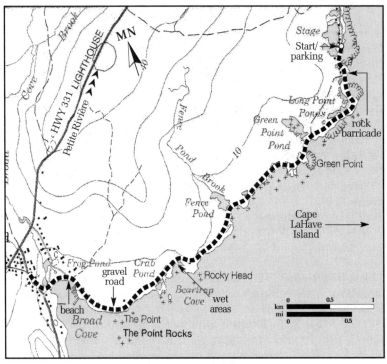

Green Bay – Broad Cove

get through the deep, soft sand, so drive no further.

The last set of cottages is on the rocky promontory of Green Point, 400 m/yd later. From here you can look back into Green Bay. Rissers Beach and the Provincial Campground are easily visible, as is the long, flat line of dunes on Crescent Beach. At the end of the cottages, you will encounter a barricade of rocks, with signs that inform you that pedestrian traffic only is permitted beyond this

point. Beyond here, the hike follows the coastline for the next 4 km (2.5 km), with wonderful scenery and numerous small sandy beaches. Much of the old track heads through sand, and your feet will sink deep into the soft footing.

You will notice frequent signs of human intervention. ATVs have cut many trails into the interior and parallel to the old road, but you should have no difficulty following your route. You may also notice hoof prints in the trail, especially clear in the harder packed surfaces. Fire rings are quite common, and every white spruce thicket seems to have become a campsite.

Walking is initially quite easy. Although there are no bridges, the few tiny brooks are easily crossed either on stones or by moving to the beach and crossing there. When you reach Beartrap Cove, the ocean at high tide covers the old road. For some, this will be the place to turn back, because crossing requires either an awkward fight through thick brush or a 15 m/yd knee-high wade. Some other portions of the old road are now also submerged at high tide, perhaps evidence of Nova Scotia's slowly sinking Atlantic coastline. On the far side of this water hazard is the first building accessed from the Broad Cove direction. The trail, a little wetter in places, gently curls around "The Point" and into Broad Cove. More and more little cabins can be glimpsed through the trees on your right, and the track once again begins to look like a roadway, not a muddy path.

Once around The Point, you can see all of the picturesque village of Broad Cove, and your route becomes a gravel road. Continue 1 km (.6 mi) further into the village, past the Frog Pond, to the store near the churches, because an ice cream cone might be just the thing to celebrate the halfway point of your hike. Return by the same route.

Cautionary Notes: Wood ticks are active from April to July.

Cellphone Reception: Minimal reception that is adequate only in unpredictable spots.

Future Plans: A community group plans to develop this route as a managed trail.

Green Point, Green Bay – Broad Cove Trail. MH

Vanishing Coastline

At high tide, parts of the former cart-track that makes up the Green Bay – Broad Cove Trail are under water. This is because Nova Scotia's Atlantic coastline is disappearing.

The good news is that the overall rate is fairly slow: about 1 cm per year, as the North American continental plate slowly submerges into the ocean along the Trans-Atlantic Fault line. However, the amount of loss can vary tremendously depending upon soil types and tidal action.

The soft soils of the drumlins that cover the South Shore are particularly susceptible to erosion. During violent fall and winter storms, you can sometimes observe massive blocks of the soft hillsides crumble and fall into the sea, which can make them dangerous places to be standing. Waterfront properties built on drumlins can lose up to 2 metres of depth each year, which can make them dangerous places to build.

Liberty Lake Loop

Length: 60 km (37.5 mi) one way
Hiking time: 3 days
Type of Trail: walking path,
    dirt road, former road
Uses: hiking, cross-country skiing
Facilities: outhouses, campsites,
    firewood, garbage cans, water,
    shelter with stove
Gov't Topo Map:
    Kejimkujik 21 A/6
Rating (1-5): 5 [distance]
Trailhead GPS Reference:
    N 44° 26' 32.2" W 65° 15' 11.9"

Liberty Lake Trail, Kejimkujik National Park. MH

Access Information: From the Kejimkujik National Park entrance, drive 5 km (3 mi) to the turnoff for Jeremys Bay Campground. Turn right and follow the road over the Mersey River. On the far side of the bridge, the road divides, with a dirt road going right. Follow it for 3 km (2 mi) to a parking lot. The trail starts at the far end.

Introduction: If you wish to go for a overnight backpacking experience in Nova Scotia, you will almost certainly find yourself on this trail. The Kejimkujik backcountry is filled with lakes, interesting vegetation, and abundant wildlife. Between Frozen Ocean and Peskawa lakes, you will be in a rarely travelled area. In most years, fewer than 100 people per year

have registered for this trip around the backcountry.

This trek can be undertaken either as part of a multi-day excursion around the entire park, with several side-trip possibilities, or as an overnight out and back hike. I have suggested camping at site 43, but this will require a full day of walking from Big Dam Lake. Sites 44 and 45 are common alternatives, especially if you plan to return along the same route.

Trail Description: The initial section is confusing; paths to Channel Lake, the canoe launch, and several campsite trails tempt the unwary, and about 500 m/yd into the walk is the junction to the Hemlock and Hard-

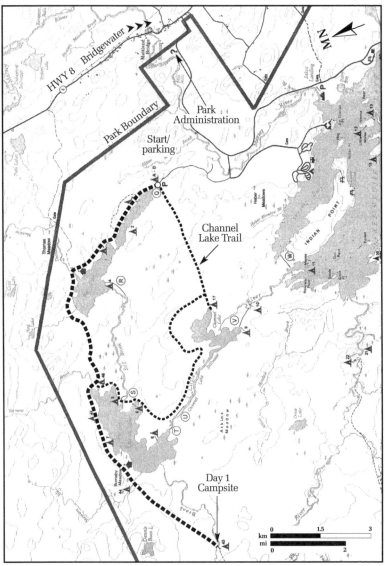

Liberty Lake Loop: Day 1

woods Trail. After this you can more fully enjoy your surroundings. The trail is well-maintained, easy walking, and quite distinct. Big Dam Lake is on your left, usually visible through the forest. Continue straight through the next junction, then, less than a kilometre (.6 mi) later, you will reach Campsite 3. As at all the prepared sites, there are outhouses available.

After nearly 4 km (2.5 mi), the trail joins a dirt road. Left leads to a warden's cabin and a dead end, so turn right. In a short distance, a small sign directs you sharply left again. A former road forms the trail for the next 4 km (2.5 mi) to Frozen Ocean Lake and another junction. Walk left for 50 m/yd and you will find Campsite 46 and, beyond that, the Channel Lake Trail. Straight ahead is a clearing and a good view of the lake. Turn right, crossing over lively Torment Brook on a footbridge, and the trail narrows to a footpath once again.

Campsite 45 marks the 12 km (7.5 mi) point of the day's walk. Beyond 45 the trail gets rockier and narrower. It also frequently moves back on a ridge away from the water's edge, and into the park's Designated Wilderness Area, which makes up 41% of Kejimkujik, almost 163 km² (63 mi²). Campsite 43, located just over the bridge at Inness Brook, suddenly appears. It is a beautiful location and a good end for the day's hike.

Day 2: Leaving Inness Brook and hiking west, the path climbs gently for the next 3 km (2 mi), but then descends towards the Northwest Branch West River. On the other side of the brook, you pass through significant pine and spruce stands, but then travel through fairly ordinary mixed forest. The trail stays reasonably level for the next several kilometres, gradually curving towards the south.

Your first clue that you are approaching Liberty Lake is a fairly messy boggy area. After several hundred metres/yards of wet feet, you can see Liberty Lake on your right. The warden's cabin is easy to spot and, although locked, has a well and outhouses for general use. About 1 km (.6 mi) past that, at the south end of Liberty Lake, is campsite 42, approximately 25.5 km (16 mi) from Big Dam.

The trail junction with the West River Trail is 4 km (2.5 mi) further. This side trail along the West River is a trip you may wish to add to extend your stay in the park. Following it to campsite 22 and back will add 13 km (8 mi) and a day to your itinerary. From this junction, the loop trail descends to cross the West River and follows lovely Red Lake Brook. Fortunately there are sturdy bridges at every crossing. Unfortunately, there is a large wet area before you cross the river that floods with every heavy rain and must be the wettest spot in the park.

The path eventually becomes a for-

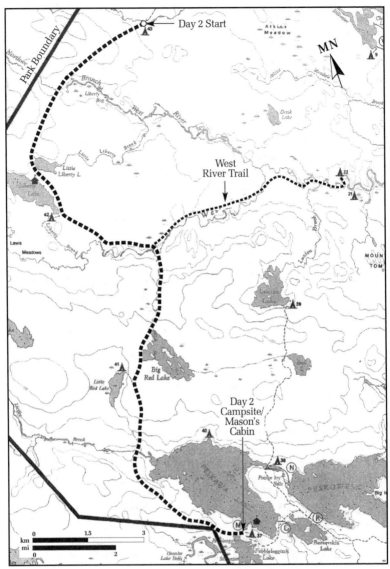

Liberty Lake Loop: Day 2

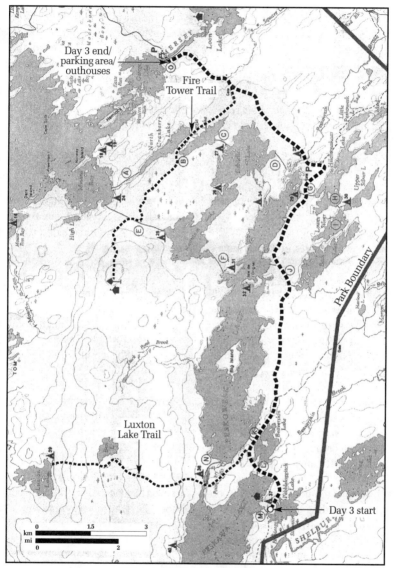

Liberty Lake Loop: Day 3

mer logging road that is generally not in very good shape. Big Red Lake is visible on your left, and, about 500 m/yd beyond, you will find the junction to campsite 41 and Little Red Lake. A large bridge crosses Lucifee Brook, and, about 200 m/yd afterward, the trail becomes a wide, dry, dirt road. Perhaps 5 km (3 mi) remain, very easy walking. Once across Lucifee Brook you have also moved out of the Designated Wilderness Area of the park. Mason's Cabin, campsite 37, and the end of the day's 23 km (14.5 mi) hike boasts a well, toilets, firewood, wood stove, indoor tables, and bunk frames. It is the perfect spot to put up your feet.

Day 3: The final day's hike of 18.5 km (11.5 mi) is a gentle walk. If you have time, venture down to Pebbleloggitch Lake and stick your arm in the water. It will disappear into the murky liquid. Much of the water that flows into this lake passes through lowlying bogs, where it picks up dissolved organic substances including tannins. The water is stained dark brown, almost the colour of tea. Many of the lakes and streams of the park are so affected.

You have numerous side-trip options, including the 14 km (8.75 mi) Luxton Lake Trail and the 9 km (4.5 mi) Fire Tower Trail. Otherwise follow the main route, mostly shaded by fine hardwoods, until the last kilometre (.6 mi), when the trail climbs to the top of a drumlin ridge that parallels the Mersey River. When it starts to turn to the right and descend, you have only about 200 m/yd remaining. The hike ends at the parking lot at Mersey River. You will need to have a car here as it is more than 20 km (12.5 mi) from Big Dam.

Cautionary Notes: The Liberty Lake Loop will take you into the interior of Kejimkujik Park where there are few services and fewer people. Find out from park officials about animal sightings and ground conditions before you start.

Mandatory registration for all overnight trips is required.

There are several sensitive environmental areas that you will pass through containing rare plants. Stay on the trail, and pick nothing.

This is tick country from April to July.

Cellphone Reception: Adequate through most of the route, but some dead areas occur between campsite 43 and Liberty Lake.

Further Information: Consider purchasing the *Backcountry Guide*, which shows all of the trails, campsites, warden cabins, and other park services. Other free park pamphlets, such as *You Are in Black Bear Country* and *Exploring the Backcountry*, are also a good idea.

Shelburne Rail Trail

Length: 22 km (13.5 mi) rtn
Hiking time: 4-7 hr
Type of Trail: abandoned rail line
Uses: hiking, mountain biking, horseback riding, cross-country skiing
Facilities: picnic tables, access to provincial park
Gov't Topo Map:
Shelburne 20 P/14
Rating (1-5): 4 [distance]
Trailhead GPS Reference:
N 43° 45' 53.7" W 65° 19' 04.0"

Access Information: The trailhead is found on King Street in Shelburne opposite the fire hall and community centre. There is a large parking area across the street from the start of the trail.

Introduction: Filled with United Empire Loyalists fleeing the newly created United States, Shelburne briefly became one of the largest settlements in North America. However, the lack of nearby agricultural lands meant that within a decade most of these people had moved elsewhere. Among these were the Black Loyalists, and many settled in nearby Birchtown.

The Halifax and Southwestern Railway, known – not always affectionately – as the "Hellish Slow & Wobbly," operated between Yarmouth and Halifax from 1907 to 1984. After the tracks were taken up, residents used the line as an unofficial walking trail, and, in 1998, the town decided to develop a 2.4 km (1.5 mi) section as a linear park. A volunteer group, the Shelburne County Trails Association, was formed to extend the trail as far as Birchtown.

Trail Description: The section of trail inside the town is lovely, with a grassy surface and sufficient foliage to provide a bit of a canopy. The path crosses several streets, but these are all signed and posts prevent vehicles from turning onto the trail. You will cross tiny Black Brook Bridge at about 1 km (.6 mi) and reach the crossing with busy Highway 3 at 2 km (1.25 mi). The bridge crossing the mouth of the Roseway River is only 500 m/ yd further, where there is an attractive view of Shelburne Harbour to your left.

On the far side of the Roseway, the trail surface becomes a little rougher, more of a natural surface. But it is an excellent walking path, wide enough for two and dry throughout the year. Many houses are close to the path here and 700 m/yd beyond the river you will find the road leading into Islands Provincial Park. I recommend this as an interesting side trip, or a des-

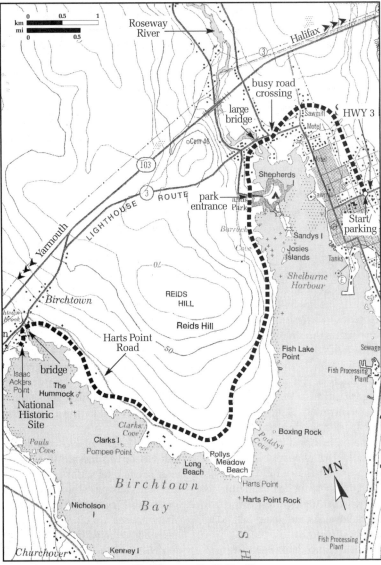

Shelburne Rail Trail

tination if you wish a shorter walk. From the end of the park, there are excellent views of the town on the opposite side of the harbour, and, when open, you will find outhouses, picnic tables, and water. In addition, little black and white domestic rabbits run free on the grounds, quite an enjoyable sight. If you choose to turn around here, you will have completed between 8 and 10 km (5 and 6 mi).

Beyond the park the trail curves around large Reids Hill and for the next several kilometres remains in featureless forest, with only occasional glimpses of the ocean available to the left. Not until nearly 7.5 km (4.75 mi) into the hike do you encounter the end of the Harts Point Road, a dirt track that the trail now parallels. At 8.5 km (5.25 mi), the trail crosses the road, and there is a wonderful old field to the left 400 m/yd later which provides views of Birchtown Bay. In the fall, this pasture is golden with ripening grasses, and looking at the old unpainted, wooden barn by the ocean made me feel as if I had been transported 100 years into the past.

The trail treadway is now surfaced with wood chips, and soon you begin

Black Loyalists

After the American Revolution, large numbers of the colonists who remained loyal to the British Crown were forced to leave the new republic. Almost 19,000 settled in Nova Scotia, overwhelming the 20,000 people already living here. Nearly 3500 settled in Annapolis County, among these nearly 500 Black Loyalists. Some of them were slaves accompanying their exiled masters, but most were freed men and women. As occurred elsewhere in Nova Scotia, the best lands in the fertile areas went to influential whites and military loyalists. Blacks, when their claims were eventually processed, were usually given smaller lots in less desirable locations.

With a population of more than 1500, Birchtown became the largest settlement of free blacks outside Africa. There were 649 male heads of families registered in Birchtown, but, because of bureaucratic incompetence and racial inequality, only 184 heads of families ever received the promised Crown land. Furthermore, the size of the Black Loyalists' grants measured an average of 34 acres – far less than what white Loyalists received.

Other Black Loyalists settled and made communities at Brindley Town (near Digby), Little Tracadie (Guysborough County), Preston (Halifax County), Annapolis Royal, Halifax, and Saint John, N.B. In the eight years that followed the Black Loyalist settlement in Lower Canada, the communities suffered many hard times. Shelburne, Nova Scotia, became the location of the first race riot in North America in 1784.

to cross the driveways of new houses built beside the bay. At about the 10 km (6 mi) point, the path crosses the road again, near house #70, and it reaches the small railway bridge crossing Ackers Brook 500 m/yd later. You are in the middle of the community, and it is quite open with houses all around and wide views. Highway 103 is barely 20 m/yd to your right. The trail reaches Birchtown Road 200 m/yd beyond the bridge.

For the final 300 m/yd, leave the tracks and turn left onto the dirt road. You will reach the turnaround point of the hike, 11 km (6.75 mi) from the start, at the site of the old Black burial ground in Birchtown. Here you will find a National Parks and Historic Site monument, erected in 1996, and picnic tables in a grassy field overlooking Birchtown Bay. Rest and eat your lunch, then retrace your route to return.

Cautionary Notes: Wood ticks are active from April to July.

Busy Highway 3 must be crossed, use caution.

Hunting is permitted in woods next to this trail. Wear hunter orange in the fall.

Cellphone Reception: Adequate reception at the start which declines as you approach Birchtown and may be inadequate to make or receive calls.

Future Plans: This hike will eventually connect to a trail extending from Halifax to Yarmouth and become an addition to the Trans Canada Trail.

Further Information: The town of Shelburne produces a brochure profiling its 2.5 km (1.5 mi) section.

The Hawk

Length: 8.5 km. (5.25 mi) rtn
Hiking time: 2-3 hr
Type of Trail: old cart track, beach
Uses: hiking
Facilities: garbage cans, out-
  house, picnic tables
Gov't Topo Map:
  Sable Island 20 P/5
Rating (1-5): 2
Trailhead GPS Reference:
  N 43° 24' 56.6" W 65° 36' 52.0"

Access Information: From Shelburne, follow Highway 103 which at Exit 27 becomes Highway 3 south for 39 km (24.5 mi) to Cape Sable Island. Turn left onto Highway 330 and drive 16 km (10 mi) to Hawk Road. Turn right, 2 km (1.25 mi) later turn left onto New Road. The parking area is 500 m/yd further.

Introduction: If you are a birdwatcher, then The Hawk is one place you must visit. Considered possibly the finest birding site accessible by foot in Atlantic Canada, The Hawk enjoys an unparalleled diversity of bird species at any time of the year. As the southernmost tip of the province, and on one of the great migratory bird routes of North America, Cape Sable Island is a stopping place for many regulars and an endlessly surprising variety of rare and stray species blown

The Hawk. ᴍʜ

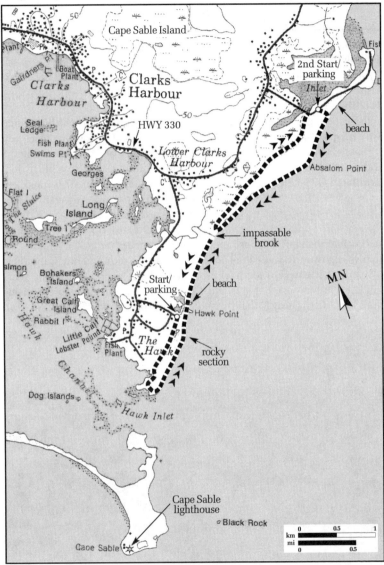

The Hawk

in off the stormy Atlantic Ocean. Migrating shorebirds gather here in great flocks in the spring and fall. Snowy owls often choose its windswept grasses as an ideal home for the winter.

The Hawk is also an example of the casual and unintended destructiveness of human activity. The dunes here, still impressive and dramatic, once rose almost 40m/yd above the high water – the highest dunes in Canada. By 1829, sheep released by the settlers to graze on the grasses that covered the dunes, and protected them from erosion from the vicious winds, had reduced the dunes to half their former height.

Trail Description: The view at the trailhead is simply incredible. Directly ahead is the ocean, dotted with tiny, rocky islands and alive with birds. To the right, you can see Cape Sable Lighthouse, on most days hard at work warning vessels of the many sandbars waiting to ground the unwary mariner. An old vehicle track heads in that direction, and is worth following as it works through the low vegetation covering Hawk Point. The road surface alternates between stony cobble and grass, and the track runs behind and lower than the beach to your left. The houses of the community are close on your right, and, as you continue, the views of Hawk Inlet, Black Point, and Fish Inlet open before you.

The trail emerges on the sandy beach at the tip of Hawk Point facing the lighthouse 1 km (.6 mi) from the start. Turn left, and follow the beach as it works around the point and heads back towards the start. All of the view is out to sea now. There will prob-

Dune Systems

Dunes are sand deposits on beaches that develop into a series of one or more ridges through wind and wave action and become stabilized by the growth of American beach grass. New dune ridges develop on the seaward side depending upon the sediment supply, the pace of erosion, and the rate of sea level rise.

All sand beaches have some measure of dune systems, although beaches on the Atlantic coast of the mainland tend to be retreating landward too rapidly for full successional series development.

The fragile grasses that populate the dunes are essential to its survival. Many provincial beaches and other protected sites have extensive boardwalks to prevent human passage that can quickly kill the plants, causing more rapid sand erosion. Please stay on these boardwalks at all times.

ably be many species of shorebirds skittering over the sand. If the weather is clear, you may notice a white dome in the distance to the east. This is the Department of Naval Defence radar installation at CFS Baccaro, more than 15 km (9.5 mi) distant.

About 150 m/yd before reaching the car, the beach narrows and you must scrabble over a short rocky section. Continue past your start; a wide, flat beach stretches before you with the fish plant and Donald Head beckoning in the distance. Hundreds of gulls and other birds speckle the sand, reluctantly moving aside as you approach, muttering their displeasure. Unfortunately, a small tidal brook, too deep and broad to ford, bisects the beach after little more than 1 km (.6 mi). You have no choice but to retrace your steps, having walked 4.5 km (2.75 mi) by the time you reach your car again.

If you wish to extend your walk, and maybe sight more bird species, return to Highway 330 and turn right, driving 2 km (1.25 mi), then turning right onto the Donald Head Road. You will find another parking area on the right 1.6 km (1 mi) later. There is an outhouse near the road, and pic-nic tables can be found on the beach. From here you may walk the beach in the other direction, 2 km (1.25 mi) until you reach the opposite side of the brook dividing the walk and must turn around. There is also a vehicle track behind the dunes running parallel to the beach, so you may vary your return slightly.

Cautionary Notes: Wood ticks are active from April to July.

The Hawk experiences high winds and extreme conditions much of the year. Hikers should always expect lower temperatures, and should avoid the ocean's edge in stormy and high water conditions.

Cellphone Reception: Adequate reception on both trails.

Thomas Raddall Provincial Park / Port L'Hebert

Length: 7 km (4.5 mi) rtn
  (Thomas Raddall)
  3 km (2 mi) rtn (Port L'Hebert)
Hiking Time: 1-2 hr
Type of Trail: gravelled paths,
  sandy beach, natural footpath,
  beach, road (Thomas Raddall)
  walking paths, boardwalks
  (Port L'Hebert)
Uses: hiking, biking
Facilities: picnic tables, benches,
  garbage cans, outhouses,
  showers, camping, play-
  ground, payphone, pop
  machine (Thomas Raddall)
  outhouses, picnic tables,
  water, benches, garbage cans
  (Port L'Hebert)
Gov't Topo Map:
  Port Mouton 20 P/15
Rating (1-5): 2
Trailhead GPS Reference:
  N 43° 49' 49.9" W 64° 53' 05.4"
  (Thomas Raddall)
  N 43° 52' 27.8" W 64° 57' 47.4"
  (Port L'Hebert)

Access Information:

Thomas Raddall: Drive approximately 29 km (18 mi) southwest of Liverpool on Hwy 103, and 4 km (2.5 mi)

*MacDonald Cemetery, Thomas Raddall
Provincial Park.* MH

down East Side Port L'Hebert Road.
Turn left into the Thomas Raddall
Provincial Park and follow the dirt
road for 3 km (2 mi) to the administrative building. Turn right for 750
m/yd to the day-use parking area.

Port L'Hebert: Drive west along Highway 103 from Liverpool towards Yarmouth. Approximately 40 km (25 mi)
from Liverpool, a large road sign indicates the parking lot and the start
of the trail.

Introduction:

Thomas Raddall: I first walked through
the proposed park in August 1994. Because of budget concerns, it was un-
certain whether it might ever open. A

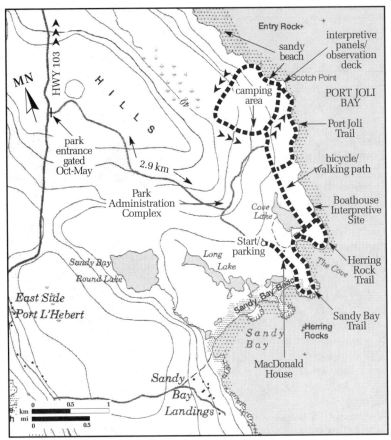

Thomas Raddall Provincial Park

community association was formed to operate the campground with assistance from the Department of Natural Resources. Thomas Raddall, which opened in 1997, is 678 ha (1,675 acres) featuring a variety of natural habitats including tremendous coastal scenery and excellent white sand beaches. The park has day-use picnic facilities, but also features 43 car campsites and eight walk-in tent sites.

Port L'Hebert: Bowater Mersey Paper Company owns and manages more than 304,000 ha (755,000 acres) of land in western Nova Scotia to sup-

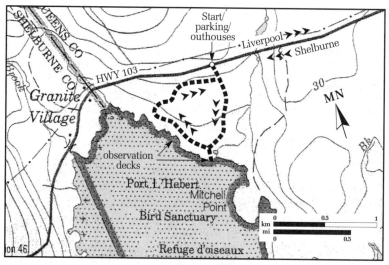

Port L'Hebert

port its newsprint and lumber manufacturing operations. To celebrate its 50th year of operation in 1979, Bowater Mersey constructed a small public nature park on land they owned near the Atlantic Ocean. This "Pocket Wilderness," as they called it, was so popular with the public that they have built several others throughout southern Nova Scotia.

Trail Description:

Thomas Raddall: You begin on a wide multi-use trail. At 200 m/yd you will reach historic MacDonald House and a cemetery where there are interpretive panels. Just past this spot is a trail junction; continue right towards Sandy Bay Beach, 250 m/yd

further. At the beach you will find a picnic area, outhouses, interpretive panels, and an extensive boardwalk over the dunes down to the water's edge.

The path turns left along the beach, and, at the end of the sand, you will find a sign indicating the Sandy Bay Trail. This narrow footpath works around a headland for 700 m/yd where it reconnects with the Cove Lake Multi-use Trail. Turn right and follow this as it skirts another beach to the start of the short Herring Rock walking trail. This traces the perimeter of another small headland and leads to the Boathouse Interpretive Site.

Back on the Cove Lake Trail, slightly more than 2 km (1.25 mi) into the walk, turn right and follow the winding route as it passes through thick forest close to small Cove Lake. One kilometre (.6 mi) later, a sign marks the start of the 1 km (.6 mi) Port Joli Trail. Turn right, and follow the tiny footpath through the many dead trees festooned with old man's beard. The path reaches the ocean within 200 m/yd and then follows the magnificent coastline for the remaining 800 m/yd to Scotch Point. The path rejoins the multi-use trail; turn right for 100 m/yd to find a large deck with several interpretive panels overlooking Port Joli. From here, follow the beach northwest. If you choose, you can continue following the sandy shoreline for several kilometres. A footpath exits into the woods on your left near a small stream only a few hundred metres/yards later. It heads away from the ocean, winding through the rocky terrain and emerges onto the park road near the walk-in camping area after a delightful meander of slightly more than 1 km (.6 mi).

To return to your car, either follow the roads through the camping area and past the park administration building, or turn left to find Scotch Point and retrace the Port Joli Trail. When it ends on the Cove Lake Multiuse Trail, follow that back to MacDonald House.

Port L'Hebert: The large parking lot sits beside Highway 103. Wheelchair-accessible washrooms are on the Yarmouth (west) side of the lot; the trail starts on the Liverpool (east) side. At the trailhead are several picnic tables and a water pump as well as a guest book. Make sure that you sign it. The path is very easy walking, dry and hard packed. Wet areas are covered by boardwalks, and the standard of maintenance is very high. Although the trail is not wheelchair-accessible, everyone else should find it easy going. Designed as a loop, the complete 3 km (2 mi) must be traversed to return to the parking lot.

Few details are required for this simple walk; the first section winds through a hardwood stand filled with huge granite boulders. These massive rocks, called "erratics," were scoured out of the bedrock by the advancing glaciers, then left behind like litter as the ice receded. After about a kilometre (.6 mi), the trail enters into a grove of softwoods on the coastal fringe and follows the shoreline, mostly inside the treeline, as it begins its return to the parking lot. Any one of the many game trails to the water's edge will provide you with wonderful views of the waters of Port L'Hebert.

During the last 500 m/yd, where the route parallels the highway, you might hear traffic noises, but they should not intrude overly much, and they pass quickly. All too soon you arrive back at the loop intersection. Turn left to return to the parking lot.

Cautionary Notes: Wood ticks are active from April to July.

Cellphone Reception: Adequate reception on both trails.

Further Information: The Department of Natural Resources publishes a brochure for Thomas Raddall Provincial Park. Bowater Mersey puts out several free brochures detailing the various conservation areas, pocket wildernesses, and recreational sites on its lands.

Thomas Raddall

OCM

Three-time recipient of the Governor General's Award for Literature, Thomas Raddall was born in 1903 in Hythe, Kent, England. He moved to Nova Scotia with his parents in 1913, served in the Canadian Merchant Marine from 1919 until 1921, and then went to Sable Island as a wireless operator from 1921 until 1922. In 1923, he came to Liverpool to serve as the accountant for pulp and paper mills on the Mersey River. In 1927, he married Edith Margaret Freeman, and, in 1938, became a full-time writer.

For distinguished service to Canadian literature, he was made an Officer of the Order of Canada and a Fellow of the Royal Society of Canada. In addition to the Governor General's Awards, he received the Gold Medal of the Royal Society of Canada, and the Gold Medal from the University of Alberta. Dalhousie University, the University of King's College, Saint Mary's University, and Saint Francis Xavier University all presented him with honorary degrees.

Thomas Raddall had a lifelong affection for this region of Nova Scotia. He died in 1994.

Wedgeport Nature Trail / Chebogue Meadows

Length: 5.4 km (3.4 mi) rtn
(Wedgeport)
5.5 km (3.5 mi) rtn
(Chebogue)
Hiking Time: 1-2 hr
Type of Trail: forest path, dirt
road, rocky beach
(Wedgeport)
walking paths, boardwalks
(Chebogue)
Uses: hiking
Facilities: benches, washrooms,
lookoff towers
Gov't Topo Map:
Pubnico 20 P/12 (Wedgeport)
Yarmouth 20 O/16 (Chebogue)
Rating (1-5): 1
Trailhead GPS Reference:
N 43° 42' 44.0" W 65° 58' 57.1"
(Wedgeport)
N 43° 53' 28.3" W 66° 03' 15.5"
(Chebogue)

Access Information:

Wedgeport: The trail begins at the
Sport Tuna Fishing Museum at the
Tuna Wharf in Lower Wedgeport, almost to the very end of the long, slim
finger of land that is home to so many
fishers and their families. From Starrs
Road in Yarmouth, near its junction

Wedgeport Trail. MH

with both Highways 101 and 103, it
is almost exactly 20 km (12.5 mi) to
the museum along Highway 334.

Chebogue Meadows: From the junction of Starrs Road and Highway 340
in Yarmouth, drive 6 km (3.75 mi)
along Highway 340 toward Corber-
rie. A sign advises that you are 800
m/yd from the park, but, at the parking lot, the sign is set in from the
road and is easy to miss. Look on
your right, just where the overhead
power lines cross the highway.

Introduction:

Wedgeport: This is an ideal trail for a

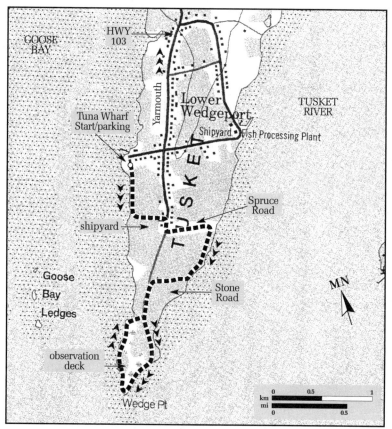

Wedgeport Nature Trail

family walk. There are very few and quite gentle hills, and the trail can be undertaken in smaller sections if 5 km (3 mi) is too much. However, this is not suitable for those wanting a challenging hike. Bring your binoculars and a bird book, because there is a great deal of both natural and human activity all around you. Walking near dusk, there was an unending procession of fishing boats on their way to the dock. Several species of duck can be heard, and occasionally observed, swimming around the marsh.

Chebogue Meadows: This is an interesting and informative outdoor educational opportunity, providing

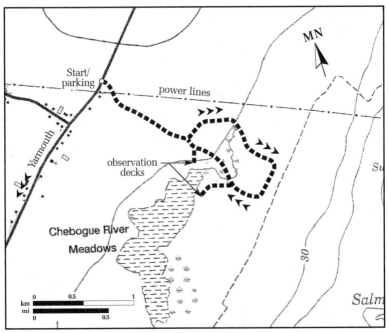

Chebogue Meadows

valuable insights into both the natural and the managed forests of Nova Scotia. A number of interpretive panels have been erected at different locations in the park where various habitats are found. The panels describe the characteristics of each habitat type, and go on to explain their value to different species of wildlife. Worthwhile for the walk and the scenery, the many interpretive panels make it particularly helpful for people like myself, who want to know more about the woods where they are hiking.

Do not be too nervous if you hear rifle fire even when it is not hunting season. The Southwestern Nova Scotia Muzzle Loading Rifle Range is less than 2 km (1.25 mi) away and always seems to be busy.

Trail Description:

Wedgeport: The walk begins at the Tuna Museum, almost on the water's edge, crossing a small field and entering white spruce forest. The first interpretive panel, just inside the tree-line, outlines the known history of this former farm site. Winding through the woods on small bridges and boardwalks over wet spots, the trail passes by the edge of a clear-cut and, 150 m/yd further, skirts a Christmas tree planting. Shortly after this, the path emerges from the woods and joins a dirt road. Signs point left, up the hill, and you pass through the middle of the LeBlanc Brothers Boat Shop, cutting between the yard's buildings, the moulds, and sections of fishing boats under repair.

This path joins the main road where the pavement ends. There is another parking area, and two possible routes. I recommend turning left and following Spruce Road down to the shores of Lobster Bay. At the water's edge, another interpretive panel describes the Tusket Estuary System, which extends inland for 19 km (12 mi). Turning right and following the shoreline takes you to the first bench, and another interpretive panel. The path gently curves towards the tip of Wedge Point.

Before you reach that spot, however, the main road reaches the shore. There is another interpretive panel and an elevated observation stand, permitting a better view of many of the 350 Tusket Islands. The trail follows the coastline on the sandy and rocky shore. In the middle of Wedge Point is a fine salt marsh, home to several varieties of waterfowl, with another observation deck and four

more interpretive panels describing the diverse habitats packed into this small area.

After a quick march through a smelly patch of eel grass, you reach the main road again, where you will find a washroom. From here, hike back into Lower Wedgeport and the Tuna Museum where you left your car, a pleasant and picturesque afternoon's stroll.

Chebogue Meadows: The path starts in the clearing under the power lines. About 25 m/yd in, you will find a large map showing the route and the location of the interpretive stations. This first section of the trail is gravelled, wide, and has long boardwalks over wet areas. It is well signed, with rectangular red metal markers affixed to the trees. Yellow is used for the return trip.

Before the first kilometre (.6 mi), the trail becomes more challenging walking, with numerous small rocks and jutting roots. When you reach the trail junction, turn left, and, just beyond it, you find interpretive stations 1 and 2 and a bench if you need to sit. Continuing a short distance through softwoods, you reach the Chebogue River. Crossing on a long boardwalk, you will notice the large, open sedge meadows on your right. Moving uphill onto drier ground, you will find stations 9 and 10. Station 10A is found just before the trail makes a 90° turn to the right. A fence on your left should keep you from accidentally following a former logging road.

Coming down the hill towards the river, you will encounter a side trail on your left, a 450 m/yd diversion over a small ridge which brings you to an observation deck overlooking open wetlands. Some of the trail's best viewing is found here. Returning to the main loop and re-crossing Chebogue River, you will find another viewing platform situated beside the marsh. A few hundred metres/yards beyond the viewing platform, the trail re-enters the woods and completes the loop. Your final kilometre (.6 mi) is over the route you followed in.

Cautionary Notes: A sign at the start of the Chebogue Meadows Trail warns users to wear hunter orange from September 15 to February 15.

This is tick country from April to July.

Cellphone Reception: Adequate reception on both trails.

Caribou – Munroes Island Provincial Park. MH

The Sutherland Steam Mill, Denmark. MH

Cape George

Length: 12 km (7.5 mi) rtn
Hiking Time: 4-6 hr
Type of Trail: former road,
  walking path
Uses: hiking, cross-country
  skiing
Facilities: garbage cans, benches
Gov't Topo Map:
  Cape George 11 F/13
Rating (1-5): 4 [steepness]
Trailhead GPS Reference:
  N 45° 50' 23.7" W 61° 55' 39.7"

Access Information: From Antigonish, drive 29 km (18 mi) north on Highway 337. A road sign indicates the trailhead and the parking area on the right. You will start from the Heritage School, trailhead TH1.

Introduction: Cape George was originally named Cape St. Louis, probably by Nicolas Denys, the noted diarist who was the French Governor of this area in the middle of the sixteenth century and resided in Nova Scotia for many years. In the late 1700s, Scottish settlers from the Pictou area moved into the Antigonish Highlands, which they found reminiscent of the old country. During the American Revolution, United Empire Loyalists also settled here. The Cape George region is made up of picturesque farming and fishing communities, crystal cliffs, and beautiful sandy beaches.

The tip of Cape George consists of 100 m (330 ft) cliffs, scoured by strong ocean currents. The first lighthouse was built in 1861 and is still an important navigational aid. A short hiking trail leads to the lighthouse, where there are tremendous views of the Northumberland Strait and Prince Edward Island to the west and Cape Breton Island to the east.

This hiking trail system opened in September 2000. Designed as a maze system with interconnecting paths, a wide variety of options of varying length can be selected. I have profiled one, fairly long, full-day hike.

Trail Description: The slender footpath crosses the highway and follows a creek inland through thick vegetation for 200 m/yd to junction A, where, as with every junction, there is a map of the trail system and signs indicating time and distance to the next intersection. Turn left, heading towards F, 2.7 km (1.75 mi), and you will immediately begin to climb. The path is not an improved surface, but only a narrow clearing through the trees. Occasional red paint flashes on trees mark the route. This first section is quite attractive, mostly thick white spruce with a sphagnum carpet beneath. A brook is on the left, at

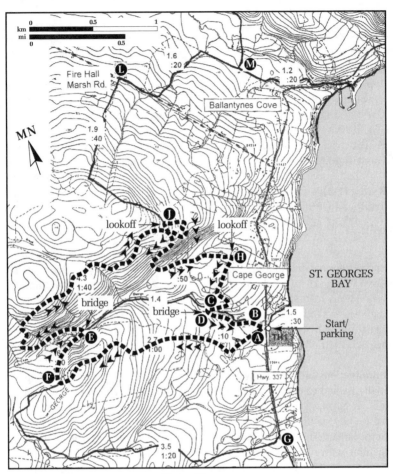

Cape George

the bottom of a little gully. After 500 m/yd, the trail leaves the brush and moves onto a woods road, still gently climbing. At 1.2 km (.75 mi), keep straight and do not follow the more distinct left fork. Watch for wooden stakes painted orange as trail markers.

The path narrows as you climb, until it leaves the old road on a new route at 500 m/yd. Ferns completely cover the forest floor among the young hardwoods, and the path circles around a knoll to end at F. Turn right toward E, 600 m/yd of meandering pathway away and (finally) downhill. The ground to the left is swampy and there are open ponds. Gravel has been spread on the trail in places and puncheons – small log walkways – traverse the worst spots.

At E, 3.5 km (2.25 mi) into the walk, turn left towards I, 4.3 km (2.75 mi) away. The path works back around the open meadows on the left, then turns to climb the steep hillside for the next kilometre (.6 mi), the most challenging section of the hike. The remainder of this section follows the ridgeline, and several clearings provide views northeast of St. Georges Bay and the Creignish Hills on Cape Breton Island. The trail contours around the hardwood ridges, then crosses numerous softwood-choked stream gorges and ravines. As you approach I, the vegetation begins to thin, and the junction itself is in a clearing which provides wonderful views.

From here, turn left and follow an old woods road towards J, walking across an open hillside with Highway 337 and the community of Ballantynes Cove visible below you. From J, an alternate exit is available by following L, a 2 km (1.25 mi) walk ending at the fire hall. Instead, turn right and drop down the slope, then loop back up the hillside to return to

I, having completed 9 km (5.5 mi) of difficult trekking. From I, head towards H, 1.3 km (.8 mi) downhill, passing into a deep, narrow ravine and across a series of puncheons through spruce and sphagnum. The junction is in a field with good views of Cape George, and there are picnic tables by the edge of the forest. The 600m/yd to C starts through a grassy field, but ends in a steep ravine switching back and forth down the hillside. Continue upstream the 100 m/yd to D, crossing the brook on a sturdy bridge and climbing again on the far side. Turn left at the intersection, heading downstream on the hillside above the brook 400 m/yd to B. The last section descends to water level, and, looking left at the intersection, you will notice an interpretive panel. The wooden ruins located here are the remains of the first North Shore scout camp.

From here, the remaining walk follows the brook, on the left, at the bottom of the ravine. This is a lovely sylvan experience, and it is unfortunate that only 300 m/yd remain until you return to intersection A, and 200 m/yd further to the trailhead at the schoolhouse.

Cautionary Notes: Hunting is permitted on nearby lands. Exercise caution during the fall, and wear hunter orange garments.

Cellphone Reception: Adequate at

the trailhead and on the hilltop and ridges, but inadequate in low-lying areas.

Further Information: A brochure is available from the local tourist bureau.

Future Plans: Additional hiking trails will be developed as landowner permission is obtained, and a much larger interconnected system is envisaged.

Caribou — Munroes Island Provincial Park

Length: 11.5 km (7.25 mi) rtn
Hiking Time: 2-3 hr
Type of Trail: sand beaches, rocky shoreline
Uses: hiking
Facilities: outhouses, washrooms, tables, water, firewood, garbage cans, supervised beach
Gov't Topo Map:
   New Glasgow 11 E/10
Rating (1-5): 2
Trailhead GPS Reference:
   N 45° 43' 19.3" W 62° 39' 25.1"

Access Information: From the Trans-Canada Highway, Highway 104, turn at Exit 22 onto Highway 106. Continue through the Pictou Rotary towards the Caribou Ferry. After 7 km (4.5 mi), take the last exit before the Prince Edward Island ferry and head east (right). Drive 3 km (2 mi) down an unnumbered road; the park and its entrance are on the left.

Introduction: The coastline bordering the Northumberland Strait between the New Brunswick border and New Glasgow is some of the most sought-after land in Nova Scotia. Ideal as summer cottage country, the gentle sandstone, siltstone, and shale of this district sharply contrast with the rugged granites of the Atlantic coastal region. The shallow channel separating the mainland from Prince Edward Island offers the warmest salt water north of the Carolinas, and its long sandy beaches ensure easy access. This is one of only three true lowland areas in the province, with the topography ranging from flat to undulating. It is also a submerged

Caribou – Munroes Island Provincial Park. MH

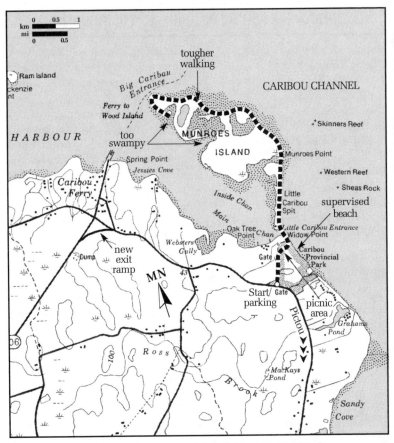

km
0   0.5   1
mi
0   0.5

tougher walking

Big Caribou Entrance

CARIBOU CHANNEL

Ram Island
ckenzie
nt

Ferry to
Wood Island

too
swampy

HARBOUR

Spring Point

Jessies Cove

Caribou
Ferry

MUNROES

ISLAND

Skinners Reef

Munroes Point

Western Reef

Sheas Rock

Inside Chan

Little
Caribou
Spit

supervised
beach

Main   Chan

new
exit
ramp

Dump

MN
43

Websters
Gully

Oak Tree
Point

Little Caribou Entrance
Widow Point

Caribou
Provincial
Park

Gate

Start/ Gate
parking

Pictou

picnic
area

Graham
Pond

06

Ross

100

MacKays
Pond

Brook

Sandy
Cove

Caribou – Munroes Island Provincial Park

coastline, the land link with Prince Edward Island having been severed by the rising ocean between 5000 and 7000 years ago. Pictou Island is a remnant of a ridge that ran through the centre of what is now the Northumberland Strait. Caribou – Munroes Island represents one of the few nat-

ural settings remaining along this beautiful coast.

This is a wonderful stroll for a lazy Sunday. The flat, wide beaches encourage dawdling, and I find it difficult to resist the urge to build a sandcastle. Except for its occasional rocky sections, this is a walk for everybody. Those not interested in hiking may always remain on the supervised beach or in the picnic area on the high ground just behind the beach.

Trail Description: This trail requires little elaboration. In essence, you just follow the shoreline. From the parking lot, a wooden stairway leads to the beach. If the park is closed, it is a 700 m/yd walk from the road to the stairs, keeping to the left track throughout. Pictou Island and Prince Edward Island may be visible to the north and Merigomish to the south. In the summer, lifeguards supervise a clearly marked section of the beach, and you will feel overdressed in your hiking gear as you walk past. Munroes Island, or Little Caribou as it was once called, is no longer separate from the mainland. As recently as the early 1980s, a narrow channel of water cut it off from Widows Point, where the picnic area is located.

For more than a kilometre (.6 mi), you walk through a beautiful exposed sandspit populated only by low grasses. Stay on the park (right) side of the beach. Footing becomes a little rockier at the point at the far end of the beach, especially in areas exposed at low tide. An impounded salt marsh is located on your left, home to ducks and sandpipers. Continuing along, whimbrels, yellowlegs, spotted sandpipers, and other shorebirds will be combing the exposed shore for dinner, and you may spot terns and gulls sitting on the rocks offshore. Another pond appears on your left, and, at high tide, you might get wet feet crossing its channel to the ocean. At low tide, however, this is only a shallow indentation through the sand. The next point beyond the pond contains the roughest walking. Practically no sand fringe exists, and the shore is a small embankment between the forest edge and water level.

The ferries connecting Wood Island, PEI, and Caribou pass very close in the channel between Caribou Island and Munroes Island. Another sandy beach fills the next cove, a thin ribbon connecting the more stable tree-covered areas. Walk to the grass fringe on top, and you will see another lagoon. I have sighted as many as 10 herons here. The final kilometre (.6 mi) rounds a wooded point with a stony beach, finishing on a grass-covered point that curves around to provide impressive views of Caribou Island, Caribou Harbour, and the ferry terminal. Although the wide beach continues beyond this point and appears to offer an easy return, the inland side of the island is a much tougher hike. Marshy banks replace the sand and stone of the strait shore, and muddy feet are certain. I recommend that you sit on the sandy beach beneath the automated light, enjoy a lunch or snack, and return along your original route.

Cautionary Notes: Many bird species, including great blue heron, nest on Munroes Island. When disturbed, herons abandon their nests and eggs, and one person walking underneath their nesting tree is sometimes sufficient to frighten them away permanently. To minimize disruption, restrict your hiking to the forest edge.

Cellphone Reception: Adequate throughout.

Fairmont Ridge

Length: 11 km (7 mi) rtn
Hiking Time: 3-4 hr
Type of Trail: woods road, footpath
Uses: hiking, cross-country skiing
Facilities: parking lot, garbage can, benches
Gov't Topo Map: Antigonish 11 E/13
Rating (1-5): 3
Trailhead GPS Reference: N 45° 41' 15.7" W 61° 54' 58.7"

Access Information: From Antigonish, drive 9.5 km (6 mi) north on Highway 337. The parking area is on the left, marked by a roadsign.

Introduction: The Fairmont Ridge Hiking Trail System, constructed by the Antigonish Hiking and Biking Trails Association, will appeal to both experienced hikers and a family of novices. Within its compact boundaries can be found lakes, fields, beaver dams, eagle nests, steep climbs, deep ravines, and mature woods. Those desiring a good trek will "enjoy" the 370 m (1200 ft) of climb over the full hike. Less experienced outdoors people will appreciate that there is a map sign found at every trail junction, and that you are never more than 800 m/yd from any one of them.

Ascending from the peaceful waters of Antigonish Harbour, Fairmont Ridge offers great vistas of Antigonish Harbour, St. Georges Bay, and Cape Breton Island from numerous locations along the route. Many options are available with this maze design of trail network. The hike I outline

Fairmont Ridge. MH

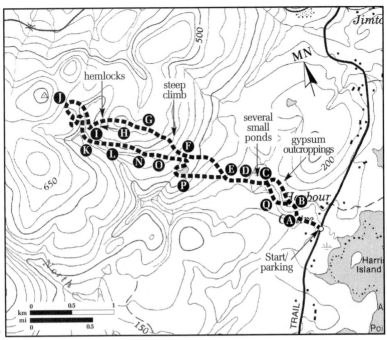

Fairmont Ridge

is created by taking the right-hand path at every trail intersection.

Trail Description: From the parking area, the path crosses an agricultural field on the farmer's road. At 300 m/yd, a sign directs you into the forest, where you drop down a stairwell and cross a small stream. On a narrow footpath beside the brook, the trail meanders to intersection B, 400 m/yd further. Keep on the right-hand junction to C, 500 m/yd away. Bright white granite outcroppings intrude, including an entire rock face

on your right. Halfway to C, the path crosses over the brook and passes through a low wet area to reach the intersection at the base of a hill. The 200 m/yd to D climbs over a small, softwood-covered ridge with good views of several small ponds and large wet areas created by beaver activity.

From D, the path to the right soon recrosses the brook and heads upstream onto drier ground. After perhaps 500 m/yd, the trail turns away from the water, and climbs the hillside into a field growing over with white spruce and, nearing intersection E, white birch. Again keeping right towards F, the view of the harbour is wonderful as you cross through a forest plantation, climbing gradually all the time. After junction F, your work begins as you climb more than 200 m (650 ft) in elevation over the next 500 m/yd to G. Your calves will be burning as you follow the old road through the thick hardwood, reaching the junction after 3.5 km (2.25 mi) of challenging hiking.

Head toward H, a 900 m/yd trek through an upland hardwood grove. Most of the climb is complete, the trail working back and forth over low ridges. In the last few hundred metres/yards, the trail begins a steep descent into a deep ravine forested in old growth red spruce and hemlock. Continue down the near vertical slope the 300 m/yd to I, which is located on the bank of a small brook. Turn right yet again, and head upstream towards J. You will find that hardwoods dominate here. The path provides a lovely trek up narrow, tiny gullies choked by deadfall with steep-sided slopes on both sides, extremely attractive and very demanding. The path crosses over the brook – there is no bridge – and climbs the steep hillside to J, 500 m/yd from I. This is by far the most rugged section of the tramp.

From J, only one option is available, following the trail 900 m/yd to intersection K. Following the ridgeline initially, the path switches back while descending the hillside and returns to the hemlock-shrouded creek bed. The 200 m/yd to L follows the creek, crossing twice, before climbing sharply to the junction. The right path to N, 600 m/yd along a narrow footpath hugging the hillside, is a lovely walk with views of the gully to your right through the hemlocks. The route is similar to O, a further 400 m/yd, though the ridge is less steep.

O is located in a small grassy field, with an excellent view of the mouth of Antigonish Harbour. From here the path drops rapidly, losing almost 100 m (330 ft) in elevation, to F at the top of the tree plantation, where you have been before. This time, however, turn right towards P. The path works its way around a beautiful small pond formed in a gypsum sinkhole, hugging the hillside and climbing sharply for short distances.

Barely 2.5 km (1.5 mi) remains, initially 600 m/yd through the Christmas tree plantation to E, then along the 400 m/yd path you have walked before to D. Keep right at this intersection, working around another small pond and granite outcroppings the 400 m/yd to Q, briefly walking on a woods road. Watch closely for directional signs. Turn left at Q towards B, passing beside another small gypsum sink pond on the right and a swampy area on your left next to the brook. Once across a tiny, unrailed wooden bridge, 400 m/yd later, the 700 m/yd remaining back to the trailhead follows the path you walked initially.

Cautionary Notes: Some sections are steep-sided and without railings.

Cellphone Reception: Adequate reception at the start, but inadequate in some hollows and in the steep-sided gullies at the back of the system.

Future Plans: Originally a trail climbing Sugarloaf was planned, but problems with private landowners prevented this. The group hopes to do so in the future, and to connect both trails.

Further Information: A brochure with a map is available at the local tourist bureau. Website: www.antigonish.com /trail.

Fitzpatrick Mountain

Length: 16 km (10 mi) rtn
Hiking Time: 4-6 hr
Type of Trail: former road,
walking paths
Uses: hiking
Facilities: picnic tables, benches,
outhouses
Gov't Topo Map:
New Glasgow 11 E/10
Rating (1-5): 4 [navigation]
Trailhead GPS Reference:
N 45° 39' 09.3" W 62° 38' 25.4"

Access Information: From New Glasgow, drive along Highway 104 until you reach Exit 22. Take Highway 106 across the Pictou Causeway to the rotary. Follow Route 376 for 5 km (3.25 mi) to Lyons Brook, then turn onto Route 256 and drive to the village of Scotsburn. The trailhead is located behind the tennis courts at Scotsburn Recreation Grounds. Look for a large sign at the edge of the woods.

Introduction: Developed by the Pictou County Trails Association in 1996, the Fitzpatrick Mountain Trail was one of the first of Nova Scotia's new trails developed by community associations. Originally formed to develop the abandoned rail line, the Pictou County Trails Association turned their attention to Fitzpatrick Mountain when legal delays prevented them from working on the rail bed. They negotiated passage with private landowners, and cleared a footpath along the crest of the mountain and through some attractive, sheltered creek valleys.

Stonehame Mountain Chalets recently opened on the slope of Fitzpatrick Mountain and helps maintain the trails for the use of their guests. Most walkers should consider turning around before the trail descends Fitzpatrick Mountain after 5.5 km (3.5 mi). The navigational difficulties past this point are substantial, and the climb back up the steep ridge is demanding.

Trail Description: The path starts at the edge of the forest behind the recreation buildings. Yellow rectangular markers on trees provide an indication of the route. Initially passing through young softwoods and crossing a field 300 m/yd from the start, the trail follows a brook up the hillside, crossing on rough bridges. At 750 m/yd, the track climbs a wonderful hillside of mature hemlock. The treadway is indistinct, so watch closely for the yellow markers, posted fairly high on tree trunks.

At 1 km (.6 mi), the trail crosses the gravel road to Stonehame Chalets, marked by a small sign, and, for perhaps 500 m/yd, you will walk

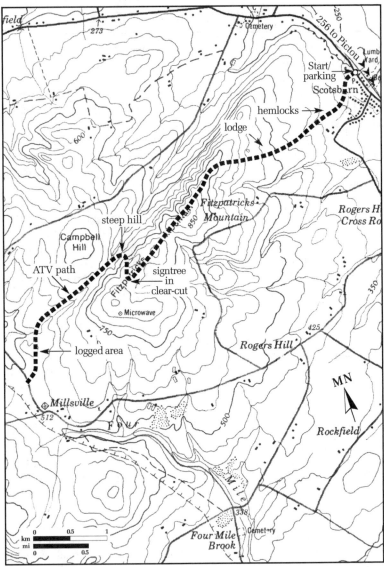

Fitzpatrick Mountain

alongside an old settler's stone wall. The climb is steady, but gradual, except for occasional drops around knolls. At 2 km (1.25 mi), you should notice cleared fields on your right as power lines pass overhead. Perhaps 200 m/yd later, the trail passes through a clear-cut area and, on the far side, follows the path of an old woods road. White spruce thickly covers the ground all around you and provides a canopy overhead. After another 400 m/yd of climb, a side trail connects to Stonehame Chalets, visible on the right. A side path on the right 200 m/yd further leads to a look-off and also connects to the chalets.

The track now appears to be used by ATVs, although the footpath diverges to the right into hardwoods 100 m/yd later. Both routes stay close as the climb continues for another 500 m/yd. Views of the lowlands should be possible through the trees on your right, and, as you continue along the ridge, frequent clear-cuts also open up the vista to the left. This is the crest of Fitzpatrick Mountain, and, for the next kilometre (.6 mi), the ATV and hiking paths will cross and recross, and the route will alternate between stands of young sugar maple and beech and clear-cuts.

At approximately 5.5 km (3.5 mi), the trail turns sharply right and descends into the valley between Campbell Hill and Fitzpatrick Mountain. A lone spruce, standing in the middle of a large clear-cut, festooned with ATV, snowmobile, and hiking trail markers, is the turning point. The microwave tower at the top of the mountain appears just ahead. Once you make the turn, the path rapidly descends the steep slope on a grassy treadway. Turn left at the first junction, then right at the next, watching for yellow markers and red arrows burned into grey wooden shingles. Approximately 500 m/yd later, the path crosses a small brook and turns left to follow the water-course. The route is now a distinct ATV trail, still descending, although more gradually, with frequent wet areas. The forest in the bottom of the gully is attractive older softwood. Another ATV trail joins from the right 400 m/yd later. A further 400 m/yd and you will reach another junction.

Those wishing to do so may continue to follow the ATV trail. It will emerge on the Millsville Road within 1 km (.6 mi). I recommend that most people choose this option. However, the walking trail, indicated by yellow markers and flagging tape, heads left on a rough footpath towards the brook. A fresh clear-cut obliterates the route for a stretch of 300 m/yd, and only a good navigator will be able to find the path on the far side, an old woods road marked by orange flagging tape. This is a pretty section, complete with a grassy treadway that parallels the brook, which is on your right. The presence of fields alerts you that you are nearing the end of the hike, and you shortly emerge beside the dirt Millsville Road where a large trailhead sign marks the turnaround point.

Cautionary Notes: The final half of the trail is very difficult to follow because of logging and the treadway is covered with branches. Be prepared to turn around if the route gets too confusing.

Cellphone Reception: Adequate reception throughout.

Future Plans: The local group would like to connect this route with paths over nearby Dalhousie Mountain.

Jitney / Samson – Albion Trails

Length: 3 km (2 mi) rtn (Jitney)
7 km (4.5 mi) rtn
(Samson – Albion)
Hiking time: 1-2 hr
Type of Trail: asphalt, gravel
Uses: hiking, biking, cross-country skiing, wheelchairs
Facilities: flush toilets, picnic tables, garbage cans, covered tables
Gov't Topo Map:
New Glasgow 11 E/10
Rating (1-5): 1
Trailhead GPS Reference:
N 45° 40' 32.3" W 62° 42' 45.4" (Jitney)
N 45° 35' 48.6" W 62° 38' 40.6" (Samson – Albion)

Access Information:

Jitney Trail: From Highway 104, drive 12 km (7.5 mi) on Highway 106 to the Pictou Rotary. Take the first exit right, West River Road, then follow it to Water Street and the town centre of Pictou, about 2 km (1.25 mi). The rail begins behind the DeCoste Centre.

Samson – Albion Trail: The trail can be accessed throughout its route, but you may wish to begin at the northern trailhead on the corner of Terrace Street and Cameron Avenue, found on the west side of the East River in New Glasgow.

Haliburton Brook Bridge, Jitney Trail. MH

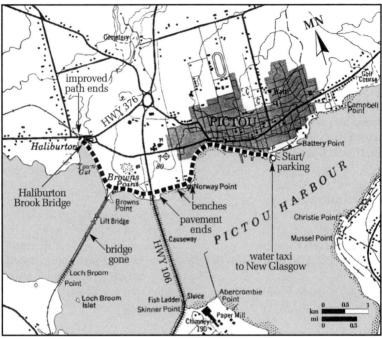

Jitney Trail

Introduction: These routes are high-quality, urban, level, walking trails, taking advantage of particularly attractive sections of an abandoned rail line. They demonstrate the possibilities of using these public rights-of-way to permit low-risk alternative transportation access into urban cores.

Jitney Trail: This path follows the route of the former Pictou Short Line from the centre of the Pictou waterfront to Browns Point, the landing site of the original Scottish settlers in

1773. The Pictou "Jitney" was a noisy diesel electric train that once carried mail, passengers, and light freight between Pictou and Oxford Junction. The Jitney consisted of a locomotive, a mail car that also carried first-class passengers, and a second car for second-class passengers.

Samson – Albion Trail: This trail follows the route of the very first Iron Railway in Canada. In 1836, the General Mining Association began construction in order to haul coal from the Albion Mines to harbour at

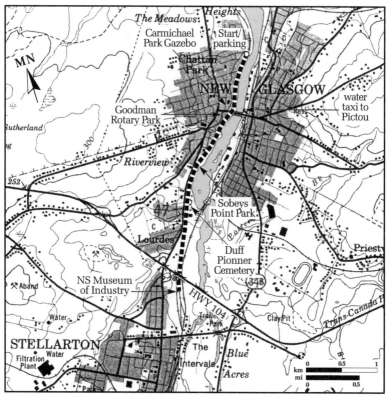

Samson – Albion Trail

Dunbar Point for loading, a distance of 6 mi (3.75 mi). A trio of steam locomotives was imported from England and the line opened in 1839. It closed in 1867. You can see one of the massive engines, the Samson, on display in the Nova Scotia Museum of Industry in Stellarton. During construction of the trail, some of the oldest railway artifacts in Canada were discovered. Musket balls, railway ties,

and shillings from 1802 and 1820 were discovered.

If you want to connect the two trails, consider the Jigs and Reels Water Taxi. This runs daily from the New Glasgow Riverfront Marina to the Pictou Marina, a trip of about slightly more than 10 km (6.25 mi) covered in about 20 minutes. The boat leaves New Glasgow at 0900, 1200, and at 1700; it leaves Pictou at 1000, 1300, and at 1800. The cost is $10 one-way, $18 for a return trip.

Trail Description:

Jitney Trail: The trail begins behind the DeCoste Centre on the waterfront. A large wooden gate marks the start, which connects with the sidewalk along the harbourfront. The first 1 km (.6 mi) of the trail is paved and wide enough for two bicycles to meet. For the first half the walk, the trail traces the perimeter of Pictou Harbour to Norway Point, where the famous Norway House, built in 1814, still stands. There are several benches along this stretch. At Norway Point, benches and an interpretive panel are found in a very attractive little grove of white and yellow birch. Pictou and the harbour across to Pictou Landing, Abercrombie Point, and the East River are spread out for view.

Beyond Norway Point, the pavement ends but high-grade gravel provides excellent footing. A few hundred metres/yards further, the trail passes underneath Highway 106. From here, you enter a wooded section and a road crosses over the trail (there are gates on the trail on either side of it). You will probably notice several houses on your left through the trees. In less then a kilometre (.6 mi), you will reach a junction. Turn right, and the trail continues for about 1 km (.6 mi), ending at Highway 376 just after crossing the Haliburton Brook Bridge. This section provides fine views of the upper harbour and the waters of the Town Gut.

Return to the junction, but take the left fork, and continue the remaining 150 m/yd to Browns Point. This is a well-developed picnic area with several tables, two interpretive panels, garbage cans, and a flush toilet with a sink and drinkable water. Browns Point is also on the water, with the remains of the Loch Broom railway bridge providing an extension and a better view of Pictou Harbour. Retrace your route to return.

Samson – Albion Trail: Start at Kinsman Lookoff Park, a small bluff overlooking the East River. There is a parking area with benches, garbage cans, and a covered picnic table. One attractive feature of the trail is that it is lighted throughout its length by antique light standards, and is wheelchair-accessible. Carmichael Park, a popular resting area for more than a century, is located at the George Street Bridge, 800 m/yd into the walk. It contains World War I and World War II monuments and a grand old gazebo where one might shelter from a shower. You cross under the busy road beneath the bridge.

Just beyond the George Street Bridge is Goodman Rotary Park, with benches, tables, a parking area, and even a launch ramp for your boat. At Sobeys Point Park, 2 km (1.25 mi) into the walk, the trail splits. The left fork climbs a small knoll where benches overlook the river. There is a plaque set into a granite block commemorating the opening of the Samson Trail on June 7, 1996.

The right fork climbs to Stellarton Road and the Duff Pioneer Cemetery, located on the site of the first church in East Pictou, built in 1787. The trail then returns to the river and heads towards the Nova Scotia Museum of Industry. The remaining 1.5 km (1 mi) will take you into the community of Stellarton. This section, named the Albion Trail, transports you underneath Highway 104 onto the grounds of the Museum, quite close to the entrance in case you want to visit. Retrace your steps to return.

Cautionary Notes: None.

Cellphone Reception: Adequate reception on both trails.

Future Plans: These trails are part of the Trans Canada Trail and will be connected to the national pathway. The Albion Trail in Stellarton is being extended beyond the Nova Scotia Museum of Industry.

Tatamagouche – Denmark

Length: 21 km (13 mi) rtn
Hiking Time: 6-8 hr
Type of Trail: abandoned rail line
Uses: hiking, biking, horseback
    riding, snowmobiling, ATV
    riding, cross-country skiing
Facilities: garbage cans, outhouses,
    picnic tables
Gov't Topo Map:
    Tatamagouche 11 E/11
Rating (1-5): 5 [distance]
Trailhead GPS Reference:
    N 45° 42' 31.9" W 63° 17' 02.0"

Access Information: From the junction of Highway 6 and Highway 311, travel approximately 1 km (.6 mi) into the community of Tatamagouche on Main Street (Highway 6). Turn right onto Station Road, and follow it to the inn and the parking area beside it. The trail runs behind the inn, which is in the former station.

Introduction: Denmark was one of many small Nova Scotia communities that relied on woodcraft and lumber for its economic survival. Using pine and maple from the distant Cobequid Hills, the Sutherland Mill used steam power to manufacture sleighs, doors, carriages, sleds, windows, and gingerbread trim from 1894 to 1958. The steam boiler provided enough power to keep pro-

duction levels up to 20% higher than competing water-powered mills. The mill is now a museum, restored by the Province to its 1894 condition. If you arrive on a "steam-up" day, you will see the saws and the boiler in operation.

This section of the abandoned rail line is a full day's hike, anchored on either end by the town of Tatamagouche and the Sutherland Steam Mill Museum. It is easy tramping, but may be longer than most people's comfort.

Trail Description: From the parking lot beside the inn, follow Station Road until it crosses the wide, gravelled treadway of the trail 200 m/yd later. Turn right, and continue 300 m/yd to the steel truss bridge crossing the Waugh River. This has been fully decked and railed, and, to your left, there are excellent views of the wide river mouth. Another 300 m/yd takes you to the busy Highway 6, which you must carefully cross.

The next few hundred metres/yards are quite attractive, as the trail passes through the only section cut into a hillside. There is a minor wet area about 100 m/yd from Highway 6, but most of the path will be in reasonably good condition. The gravelled surface is found only within Tatamagouche, while the remainder of the

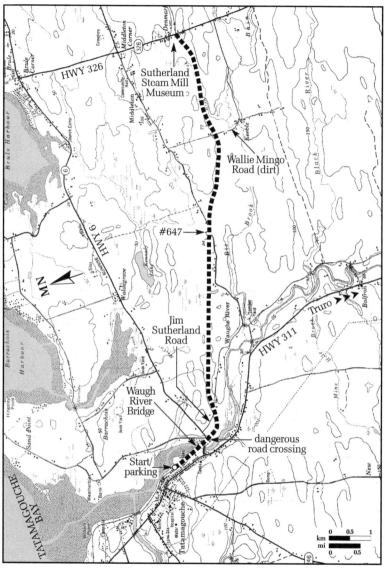

Tatamagouche – Denmark

trail is hard-packed earth. Heavy use by ATVs and off-road vehicles has created numerous potholes and ridges, so bikers should be cautious, but walkers will have no problems.

After a sharp left turn, when you might catch a glimpse of the river to your right, the trail reaches gravelled Jim Sutherland Road less than 2 km (1.25 mi) into the walk. The trail and the road intersect in the middle of a road bend, so be cautious. Several houses are nearby and the immediate area is free of vegetation. There shouldn't be any problem in safely crossing. Across the road, the path heads into a thickly forested area for the next 2 km (1.25 mi). Several ponds and meadows border on either side of the trail, but the mostly straight track enjoys few remarkable features. Halfway along, on the right, is a pond with a beaver lodge prominently in the middle, and, on the far side, you will notice some houses in the distance, part of the community of Waughs River.

At 4 km (2.5 mi), the Jr. Laurie Road, more like an old logging track, cuts over the trail. Just past this on the right is an interesting drowned forest, a pond created by beavers where the water has reached high up the trees and killed them. Forest soon gives way to a very large field on the left, with farm roads crossing at 4.5 km and 4.9 km. The barns and houses are all to your right. At 5.5

km (3.5 mi), a sizeable pond borders the embankment on the left, and extends for several hundred metres/yards. Ducks and other waterfowl seem plentiful in this particular wet area. Just before reaching the 6 km (3.75 mi) point, the paved Upper River John Road must be crossed. The trail intersects the highway next to house #647.

A long, climbing straightaway follows, broken at 6.5 km (4 mi) when a farm road crosses the trail. There are large fields visible on both sides, with a red barn and a white house on the left. Still noticeably climbing, there is an interesting large wet area on the left 1 km (.6 mi) later, where flooding from beaver activity has killed all the trees. The beavers have been trapped out and the pond drained, but many large tree trunks remain standing in the resulting meadow.

The trail crosses Wallie Mingo Road after 8 km (5 mi) of hiking. A large farmed area extends to the right, affording good views of Spidell Hill and the Cobequid Mountains. Back into thick forest, the path sweeps through several broad curves, and has been deeply rutted by vehicular uses. Barely 400 m/yd from Denmark, a large beaver pond and some houses and fields on your right are encountered. The trail reaches paved Highway 326 at the 10.5 km (6.5 mi) mark; the Sutherland Steam Mill Museum is immediately to the left.

Stop here and eat your lunch at the picnic tables on the grounds before retracing your route back to Tatamagouche.

Cautionary Notes: Highway 6 is very busy and automobile traffic has limited views and no sign warning of the crossing. Be extremely cautious.

Cellphone Reception: Adequate throughout.

Future Plans: This will be a portion of the main line of the Trans Canada Trail, a 17,100 km (11,000 mi) shared-use recreational pathway crossing the nation. It is scheduled to be officially opened in 2002.

Intercolonial Railway Station, Tatamagouche

The Intercolonial Railway ran a track from its terminus in Amherst to Pictou in 1887. Spur lines branched into industrial communities such as Pugwash, Wallace, and Malagash. Tatamagouche was located at the point where the line reached the coast of the Northumberland Strait, and a railway station was erected here in 1887. As the region's economy declined over the next decades, this station was the last sight of home for many emigrants leaving to work on the Alberta wheat fields and in the Klondike gold mines.

The rail line was torn up in the 1980s but the station has survived, having been converted into a unique inn. Former rail cars now serve as guest rooms, and a display of artifacts from the station and the station master's residence are on display inside. The Train Station Inn attracts railway enthusiasts from all over North America and Europe.

Tidnish Trail

Length: 8 km (5 mi) rtn
Hiking Time: 2-3 hr
Type of Trail: walking paths
Uses: hiking, biking, ATV riding, cross-country skiing
Facilities: outhouses, water, garbage cans, picnic tables, benches, beach, covered tables
Gov't Topo Map:
Amherst 21 H/16
Rating (1-5): 2
Trailhead GPS Reference:
N 45° 59' 47.8" W 64° 00' 32.4"

Tidnish Suspension Bridge. MH

Access Information: To reach the park, follow Route 6 from Amherst to its junction with Route 366. Continue north for 22 km (14 mi) to Tidnish Cross Roads and turn left onto a paved road. Road signs mark the entrance to Tidnish Dock Provincial Park, 400 m/yd away. Drive past the gates to the parking area nearest the ocean and follow the boardwalk to a stone monument. If the park is closed, the gates are 300 m/yd from the parking area.

You can also reach the park from the Pugwash direction, also turning off Route 6 onto Route 366.

Introduction: This is a fairly easy walk along a former rail line that has been abandoned for more than 100 years. It starts from an attractive pic-

nic ground on the shores of the Northumberland Strait, and passes through quite attractive forest to end at one of the few suspended footbridges in the province.

Families will enjoy this walk the most, but everyone will want to undertake this hike just to travel across the bridge. (It sways deliciously when you bounce up and down.)

Trail Description: You begin at a marker commemorating this location as a National Historic Civil Engineering Site (1989), the eastern terminus of the historic Chignecto Marine Transport Railway. The path of the former railroad is clear, heading southwest

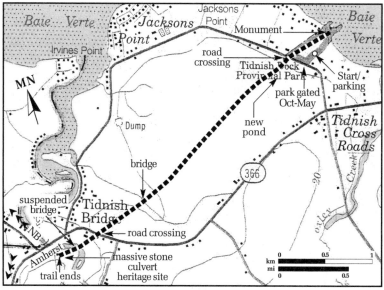

Tidnish Trail

across a lush, grassy field. Soon the footpath leaves the old rail bed, which soon becomes very wet and choked with alders. The trail parallels the rail bed on its left bank, winding through the thick brush and over a small bridge until it reaches the road, approximately 500 m/yd later. From here, turn right and cross the road bridge; a sign indicates where the trail enters the woods on the other side.

You pass very close to a house as you walk along a grass-covered ridge. To your left, the rail bed is now a pond, flooded and impounded by beaver activity. Within 300 m/yd, you will enter an area of thick white

spruce, where you will spend most of the walk. The treadway becomes an ATV track, wide enough for two to walk side-by-side as it winds between the large trees. This is a beautiful summer walk, sheltered from the sun by a dense overhead canopy of tree boughs. Numerous benches can be found overlooking the rail bed pond, and occasional steps and bridges have been constructed to assist over any difficult sections.

For the next 2 km (1.25 mi), your path passes through thick forest. After nearly 1.6 km (1 mi), an ATV trail splits from the route near a small bridge, and, 400 m/yd beyond that point, you will be able to see fields through the trees on your right. The path continues straight through the woods for a further 500 m/yd before emerging on the paved highway in Tidnish Bridge. This is Route 366, which can be quite busy, so be cautious when crossing.

On the far side, the trail continues another 200 m/yd until it reaches a magnificent suspension bridge spanning the river. A sign advises that people use the bridge at their own risk, no motorized vehicles are permitted, bicycles must be walked, and no jumping! The trail continues a further 200 m/yd, crossing over a stone culvert, which is marked by a provincial heritage site marker, and ends on a dirt road by several newer houses.

To complete the walk, retrace your route back to the park.

Cautionary Notes: There are no directional signs anywhere along the route, so people must be confident that they are following the correct path.

Cellphone Reception: Adequate throughout.

Chignecto Ship Railway Company, Cumberland, Nova Scotia. MMA

Stranger than Fiction

The Chignecto Marine Transport Railway was initially planned to be a method of reducing the sailing distance between ports on the Atlantic coastline and those on the St. Lawrence River. In 1875, Henry Ketchum, a New Brunswick engineer, proposed the construction of a 28 km (17 mi) double-tracked railway between Fort Lawrence, on the Bay of Fundy, and Tidnish Dock, on the Northumberland Strait. Ships would be transported by rail between the two locations. This would provide not only reduced sailing time but a much safer route than around the coast of Nova Scotia.

The project ran into difficulties almost immediately. The Isthmus of Chignecto is a flat area covered by marsh and bog, and was not a suitable place to build a railroad. It kept sinking into the swamp! One boggy area had to be filled 60 ft (18 m) deep with rocks to provide a solid foundation. Even with all of its technical challenges, the route was nearly completed by 1891. However, financial difficulties led to its charter being revoked by Parliament and the project died.

Several legacies remain: the rail bed, a stone culvert on the Tidnish River which has been designated a provincial heritage site, and the remains of the docks near Tidnish, which were established as a provincial park in 1982.

Wallace Bay National Wildlife Area

Length: 4 km (2.5 mi) rtn
Hiking Time: 1-2 hr
Type of Trail: walking paths
Uses: hiking
Facilities: none
Gov't Topo Map: Pugwash 11 E/ 13
Rating (1-5): 1
Trailhead GPS Reference:
N 45° 49' 43.1" W 63° 34' 01.6"

Access Information: From Pugwash, drive 8 km (5 mi) towards Tatamagouche along Highway 6. Turn left on an unnumbered road to Wallace Bay less than 1 km (.5 mi) past the Highway 368 turnoff. There is a parking lot on your left 1 km (.5 mi) along this road, just before the bridge over the Wallace River.

Introduction: Situated at the upper limit of Wallace Harbour on the Northumberland Strait, this area has long been an important migration and breeding habitat for waterfowl. In 1973, Ducks Unlimited undertook the construction of 3.8 km (2.5 mi) of dikes and five water control structures (sluices) to establish 144 ha (356 acres) of impounded wetlands. In 1980, Wallace Bay was declared a National Wildlife Area and is maintained under the Canadian Wildlife Act. Since then, there have been significant increases in both the numbers of waterfowl born here and the varieties of species inhabiting the area. Other marsh birds nest in the surrounding uplands, and even bald eagles have moved into the territory since its creation. The protected area includes more than the original wetlands, although they make up more than 75% of the total area. Of the 585 ha (1445 acres) incorporated, 17% are forest and the remainder is abandoned farmland.

What this all means is, if you like birds, this is a good place to find them. But this is also a pleasant little walk for the entire family. The trail is easy walking with practically no elevation change, particularly on the dike, and the distance is within most people's comfort level.

Trail Description: This is a loop trail and either direction will return you to the parking lot. I recommend starting your stroll on the river side. Not only is the viewing better, but the walking is easier. Your first 2 km (1.25 mi) follows the flat, unobstructed, hard-earth surface of the dike. Young white birches predominate, creating a fairly low, but relatively thick screen of leaves for most of this section of the hike. On your left are freshwater wetlands, the protected area created by the dike, and, on your right, tidal channels and salt marsh.

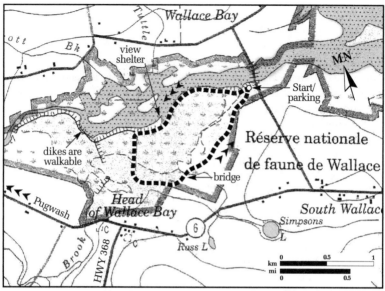

Wallace Bay National Wildlife Area

Birding opportunities are everywhere, so remember your binoculars. Near the trailhead, you will notice an elevated nesting box to your left. Originally intended for wood ducks, these boxes have proven equally beneficial to the hooded merganser population. In addition to the ducks in the water on both sides of you, the trees are likely to be homes for warblers and vireos, and the grasses and rushes are populated with several species of sparrow and the raucous red-winged blackbird. Halfway along the dike you will find an observation shelter with a sturdy bench, built by the CWS and the Wallace Area Development Association. From here, you can ob-serve both fresh and salt wetlands, although viewing is best on the river side. Across the river, the land is cleared and is open for a considerable distance. Various hawk species patrol there regularly.

Several hundred metres/yards past the observation stand are the dike forks. Continuing directly ahead you will eventually come to a dead end, but you may walk for more than 1 km (.6 mi). Instead turn left and head towards the forest. You still have water on both sides, but the vegetation is sparser and you have a wider view. Watch around this area in particular for beaver and muskrat. In late spring and summer, especially toward dusk, you will be serenaded by a froggy chorus. At the end of the dike, the trail enters a hardwood stand. From this point on, brightly painted blue jay figures affixed to trees will mark your path. As the foliage changes, so do the birds, with warblers, thrushes, and woodpeckers much in evidence.

Turning back towards the parking lot, the trail leads you through overgrown fields, an alder swamp (wet despite bridges), and finally into dense softwoods. Boreal and black-capped chickadees, nuthatches, and kinglets will be found among the spruce. The wetlands are now out of sight on your left, but not far away, as the occasional loud quacking will remind you. After a nearly 2 km (1.25 mi) trek among the widely different groves, the trail returns to the parking lot.

Cautionary Notes: Do not take dogs or other animals on this hike; they are far too disruptive to the birds and mammals inhabiting this wildlife preserve which was set aside to provide safe conditions for waterfowl breeding. You may encounter nests anywhere, including the middle of the trail. Do everything in your power not to disturb them.

Fishing, hunting, and trapping are permitted. Starting in early October, hunting season varies from year to year and between types of game. Contact the Department of Natural Resources for detailed information.

Cellphone Reception: Adequate throughout.

Further Information: The CWS has a brochure of historical and natural history information.

Wallace Bridge

Length: 8 km (5 mi) rtn
Hiking Time: 2 hr
Type of Trail: abandoned rail line
Uses: hiking, biking, horseback
    riding, snowmobiling, ATV
    riding, cross-country skiing
Facilities: garbage cans
Gov't Topo Map:
    Malagash 11 E/14,
    Pugwash 11 E/13
Rating (1-5): 2
Trailhead GPS Reference:
    N 45° 47' 14.6" W 63° 29' 10.3"

Access Information: From Wentworth, turn off Highway 4, following Route 307 for 16 km (10 mi) to the village of Wallace Station. The trail crosses the road in a clear and obvious track, almost like a gravel road.

From the village of Wallace and Highway 6, follow Route 307 for a little more than 3 km (2 mi) to Wallace Station.

Introduction: The Short Line, running between Oxford and Pictou, was a portion of the dream railway planned by Sir Sanford Fleming to connect the manufacturing centres of central Canada with the harbour of Louisbourg. The full line was never completed, but this section of operating track was opened in the 1890s.

Abandoned by CN in the 1980s,

Wallace Bridge. MH

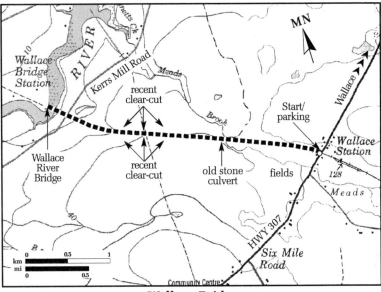

Wallace Bridge

the property was acquired by the province in 1997 and, since then, community groups have been working to develop it as a recreational trail. It has been informally used as such for many years, especially near communities such as Tatamagouche and Pictou.

This path is easy walking, but with few views until you reach the bridge. During the summer, there is little shade, so make certain you carry plenty of water.

Trail Description: Turn left, and follow the wide, level treadway in a westerly direction. Although you can see the fields on your left for a

short distance, your horizons are soon limited by a thick border of trees on both sides of the path. At 1.3 km (.8 mi), you cross an old stone culvert over sluggish Meads Brook. Beyond the brook there has been a fair amount of logging activity, and, for the next 2 km (1.5 mi), much of the forest on both sides has been thinned. The worst cutting has been along the next 1.1 km (.7 mi), and, shortly after you encounter a junction with a logging road, the woods return to a pleasing combination of older pine and spruce.

At 3.5 km (2.2 mi) into your walk, you reach a small bridge crossing the Kerrs Mill Road (dirt). To the right are a small pond and an area of old fields. Beyond this you will see the steel truss of Wallace Bridge, but it is not until you reach the structure, 300 m/yd later, that you can fully appreciate what a dramatic site it is. The structure towers above the wide Wallace River. Incredibly tall pine trees line the banks of both sides of the river. Farms can be seen on the far bank, and the bridge itself is worth examining.

The entire length of the Wallace River Bridge has been decked and railed, the work done by volunteers, most from the Route 6 Snowmobile Club and the Cumberland Trails Association. In spring and summer, osprey build a nest on the top of the steel truss, so expect to be scolded when young are nearby. Eagles commonly perch on the tall pines overlooking the river. The trail continues for a considerable distance beyond the bridge, and there is a designated parking area about 1 km (.6 mi) further. Retrace your route to return to Wallace Station.

Cautionary Notes: Except for the obvious care that should be taken when walking on the bridge itself, this is a safe walk.

There are no stores or services in Wallace Station, but there are a number of amenities in nearby Wallace.

Cellphone Reception: Adequate throughout.

Future Plans: This will be a portion of the main line of the Trans Canada Trail, a 17,100 km (11,000 mi) shared-use recreational pathway crossing the nation.

Acknowledgements

With a project like *Hiking Trails of Nova Scotia*, 8th edition, which takes several years to complete, there are so many people to thank that an author is certain to overlook many. Over the years, I have spoken to hundreds of people who either hike on, work with, or dream about trails. Each of you has made a contribution, and I wish to express my gratitude for your passion.

I would not have completed this edition if not for the help of my friends, especially Kathryn, Carrie, and Tom. They never appeared to lose their faith in me, and I cannot begin to repay their trust and love. My parents, John and Joan Haynes, have been another indispensable support. They have shown me that there is still much I can learn from them.

My employers have encouraged me tremendously, particularly the executive of the Nova Scotia Trails Federation. We work together to promote trail development and proper use of the growing network of recreational pathways throughout the province. It is an exciting time to be working in outdoor recreation, and I appreciate the opportunity to help it grow.

I must express my thanks to Hostelling International – Nova Scotia for their vision in publishing the first *Hiking Trails of Nova Scotia* book more than 35 years ago, and for trusting me to uphold the tradition of quality and dependability that they first established.

Many persons in provincial government employ, working with the community groups developing trails or with outdoor enthusiasts like myself, have contributed to making this book possible. The Nova Scotia Sport and Recreation Commission deserves special mention, as it works nonstop to support the communities who want to develop recreational trails in this province. Most of the new trails profiled in this book would not exist without their involvement.

The people at Goose Lane Editions have been remarkable. They consistently provided gentle encouragement and helpful suggestions, always appeared understanding of my situation, and demonstrated exceptional patience.

Finally, I must acknowledge the many people I have met who have purchased one of my earlier books or who have heard me speak on CBC Radio's *Information Morning*. A week does not pass without people introducing themselves and telling me of their hiking experiences. Your enthusiasm and generosity of comment always surprise and encourage me. More than anything else, the satisfaction of hearing from people who have newly discovered the joys of hiking, or who have been smitten by the singular beauty of a province that can best be discovered on foot, keeps me writing. Thank you all.

Michael Haynes
April 2002

Addresses

Bowater Mersey Information Department
PO Box 1150
Liverpool, B0T 1K0
(902) 354-3411

Cape Breton Highlands National Park
Ingonish Beach B0C 1L0
(902) 224-2306 or 285-2691

Cross Country Ski Nova Scotia
P.O. Box 3010 South
Halifax B3J 3G6
(902) 425-5450 ext. 316

Dartmouth Volksmarch Club
Box 28064, Tacoma R.P.O.
Dartmouth B2W 6E2
(902) 462-1458

Environmental Conservation Branch /
Canadian Wildlife Service
PO Box 6227
Sackville, N.B. E4L 1G6
(506) 364-5044

Extension Services
Department of Natural Resources
P.O. Box 698
Halifax B3J 2T9
(902) 424-4321

Friends of McNabs Island Society
P.O. Box 31240
Gladstone RPO
Halifax B3K 5Y1

Halifax Field Naturalists,
c/o NS Museum of Natural History,
1747 Summer Street,
Halifax B3H 3A6
(902) 424-7353

Halifax Outdoor Club
PO Box 3010 South
Halifax B3J 3G6
(902) 454-4681

Kejimkujik National Park
PO Box 236
Maitland Bridge B0T 1B0
(902) 682-2772

Les Amis du Plein Air
PO Box 472
Cheticamp B0E 1H0
(902) 224-3814 or 224-3403

Nova Scotia Bird Society
c/o Nova Scotia Museum
1747 Summer Street
Halifax B3H 3A6
(902) 424-7353

Nova Scotia Museum of Natural History
1747 Summer Street
Halifax B3H 3A6
(902) 424-7353

Nova Scotia Nature Trust
P.O. Box 2202
Halifax B3J 3C4
(902) 425-5263

Nova Scotia Trails Federation
P.O. Box 3010 South
Halifax B3J 3G6
(902) 425-5450 ext. 325

Parks and Recreation Division
Department of Natural Resources
R.R.#1, Belmont B0M 1C0
(902) 662-3030

Outdoor Recreation Centre
Halifax Regional Municipality
42 Parkhill Road
Halifax B3P 1R6
(902) 490-4539

Velo Halifax Bicycle Club
P.O. Box 125
Dartmouth B2Y 3Y2
(902) 454-299

Web Pages

Bicycle Nova Scotia: http:// bicycle.ns.ca/

Canadian Volkssport Federation: www.chebucto.ns.ca/Recreation/CVF

Climb Nova Scotia: www.peak.ca/CNS/

Canoe/Kayak Nova Scotia: www.ckns.ca

Cross Country Ski Nova Scotia: www.crosscountryskins.com/

Explore Nova Scotia: www.explorenovascotia.com

Fairmont Ridge Trail: www.antigonish.com/trail

Friends of McNabs Island Society:
www.chebucto.ns.ca/Environment/FNSN/hp-fomis.html

Halifax Field Naturalists:
www.chebucto.ns.ca/Recreation/FieldNaturalists/fieldnat.html

Halifax Outdoor Club: www.explorenovascotia.com/hoc

Halifax Regional Municipality: www.region.halifax.ns.ca

Les Amis du Plein Air: www.lesamisdupleinair.com/index.html

Musquodoboit Trailways Association:
http://home.istar.ca/~rainbow/Index.htm

Parks Canada: http://parkscanada.pch.gc.ca

Nova Scotia Bird Society: www.chebucto.ns.ca/Recreation/NS-BirdSoc

Nova Scotia Department of Natural Resources: www.gov.ns.ca/natr

Nova Scotia Museum of Natural History: http://museum.gov.ns.ca/mnh/

Nova Scotia Nature Trust: www.nsnt.ca/

Nova Scotia Trails Federation: http://novascotiatrails.com/

Nova Scotia Trans Canada Trail: www.trailtc.ns.ca/

Provincial Parks: http://parks.gov.ns.ca/

Trail Information Project: www.trails.gov.ns.ca/

TrailPaq: www.trailpaq.com/

Velo Halifax Bicycle Club: www.velohalifax.ca/

Update of 7th Edition

A number of trails profiled in *Hiking Trails of Nova Scotia*, 7th Edition, were not included in this volume. For those who own the 7th Edition, this is an update on the status of those omitted trails.

Cobequids – North Shore:
1. Beaver Mountain Provincial Park: as in 7th edition, see www.antigonish.ns.ca/ beavermountain/trails. html
2. Cutie's Hollow: as in 7th edition.
3. Gully Lake: many new confusing ATV trails. Not recommended.
4. Refugee Cove: replaced by Cape Chignecto Provincial Park.
5. Wentworth Hostel Lookoff: as in 7th edition.

South Shore – Annapolis Valley:
1. Graves Island Provincial Park: as in 7th edition.
2. Liverpool Rail Trail: as in 7th edition.
3. Mushpauk Lake : as in 7th edition.
4. Sable River Rail Trail: as in 7th edition.
5. Upper Clements Provincial Wildlife Park: the trailhead has moved inside park gates; small entrance fee required.

Central – Eastern Shore:
1. Abrahams Lake: profiled in *Trails of Halifax Regional Municipality*.
2. Duncans Cove: as in 7th edition, but overused. Not recommended.
3. Middle Musquodoboit: profiled in *Trails of Halifax Regional Municipality*.
4. Old St. Margarets Bay Coach Road: changes to first sections.
5. Pennant Point: profiled in *Trails of Halifax Regional Municipality*.
6. Queensport Road: as in 7th edition.

Cape Breton Island:
1. Cape Breton: profiled in *Hiking Trails of Cape Breton*.
2. Cape Smokey Provincial Park: profiled in *Hiking Trails of Cape Breton*.
3. Gull Cove: expanded and profiled in *Hiking Trails of Cape Breton*.
4. Highland Hill: profiled in *Hiking Trails of Cape Breton*.
5. Mabou Highlands: expanded and profiled in *Hiking Trails of Cape Breton*.
6. Meat Cove: profiled in *Hiking Trails of Cape Breton*.
7. North River Provincial Park:

profiled in *Hiking Trails of Cape Breton*.

8. Pringle Mountain: profiled in *Hiking Trails of Cape Breton*.
9. Usige Ban Falls: profiled in *Hiking Trails of Cape Breton*.
10. Whycocomagh Provincial Park: profiled in *Hiking Trails of Cape Breton*.

Cape Breton Highlands National Park:

1. Aspy: as in 7th edition.
2. Clyburn Valley: as in 7th edition.
3. Coastal: profiled in *Hiking Trails of Cape Breton*.
4. Corney Brook: as in 7th edition.
5. Fishing Cove: profiled in *Hiking Trails of Cape Breton*.
6. Franey: profiled in *Hiking Trails of Cape Breton*.
7. Glasgow Lakes: profiled in *Hiking Trails of Cape Breton*.
8. Skyline: profiled in *Hiking Trails of Cape Breton*.

Kejimkujik National Park:

1. Channel Lake: as in 7th edition.
2. Fire Tower: as in 7th edition.
3. Luxton Lake: as in 7th edition.
4. Peter Point: as in 7th edition.
5. Seaside Adjunct: similar to 7th edition, but with substantial new facilities and improved treadway.

Selected Bibliography

The following list includes most of the texts I used as background research for my hikes, although general field guides to birds, plants, animals, rocks and minerals, and geological information of Eastern North America will provide most people with sufficient knowledge about their surroundings. There is a body of excellent local publications covering all natural history areas that give more specific data, and contribute to a substantially enriching experience for both the serious and the casual outdoors person.

I have also included a few general purpose equipment guides.

Claridge, E. and B.A. Milligan. 1992. *Animal Signatures.* Nimbus Publishing and Nova Scotia Museum, Halifax.

Cunningham, Scott. 1996. *Sea Kayaking in Nova Scotia.* Nimbus Publishing, Halifax.

Davis, D.S. 1987. *Natural History Map of Nova Scotia.* Nova Scotia Museum and Department of Education, Halifax.

Davis, D.S. and S. Browne. 1996. *The Natural History of Nova Scotia.* Nimbus Publishing, Nova Scotia Museum, and Communications Nova Scotia, Halifax. 2 vol.

Donahoe, H.V. and R.G. Grantham. 1994. *Nova Scotia Geology Map.* Land Registration and Information Service and Department of Supply and Services. Halifax.

Getchell, Annie. 1995. *The Essential Outdoor Gear Manual.* Ragged Mountain Press, Camden, Maine.

Logue, Victoria. 1994. *Backpacking in the '90s.* Menasha Ridge Press, Birmingham, Alabama.

Nova Scotia Bird Society. 1976. *Where to Find the Birds in Nova Scotia.* Halifax.

Nova Scotia Department of Lands and Forests. 1980. *Notes on Nova Scotia Wildlife.* Nova Scotia Department of Lands and Forests, Truro.

Nova Scotia Department of Natural Resources. 1992. *A Map of the Province of Nova Scotia, Canada.* Formac Publishing, Halifax.

Roland, A.E. 1982. *Geological Background and Physiography of Nova Scotia*. Nova Scotian Institute of Science, Halifax.

Roland, A.E. and A.R. Olsen. 1993. *Spring Wildflowers*. Nimbus Publishing and Nova Scotia Museum, Halifax.

Saunders, Gary L. 1970. *Trees of Nova Scotia*. Nova Scotia Department of Lands and Forests, Halifax.

Saunders, Gary L. 2001. *Discover Nova Scotia: The Ultimate Nature Guide*. Nova Scotia Museum and Nimbus Publishing. Halifax.

Tufts, R. 1986. *Birds of Nova Scotia* (3rd edition). Nimbus Publishing and Nova Scotia Museum, Halifax.

Zinck, Marion. 1998. *Roland's Flora of Nova Scotia*. Nimbus Publishing and Nova Scotia Museum, Halifax

Index

C

Q

R

S

T

ALSO AVAILABLE from Goose Lane Editions

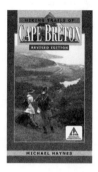

Hiking Trails of Cape Breton, Revised Edition
MICHAEL HAYNES

A revised edition of the popular guide, which includes maps, photographs, GPS coordinates, cellphone coverage, and entertaining descriptions of 56 beautiful Cape Breton trails.

0-86492-350-3 / $16.95 pb
302 pp / 4.25 x 7.25
maps, photographs, index, bibliography

Trails of Halifax Regional Municipality
MICHAEL HAYNES

Twenty-five beautiful, well tended, easily accessible trails scattered throughout Halifax Regional Municipality.

0-86492-298-1 / $12.95 pb
127 pp / 5 x 7
maps, photographs, index, bibliography

A Hiking Guide to the National Parks and Historic Sites of Newfoundland
BARBARA MARYNIAK

An enchanting and informative guide to more than 50 trails in Newfoundland's national parks and historic sites; includes maps and trail descriptions.

0-86492-150-0 / $14.95 pb
319 pp / 4.25 x 7.25
maps, photographs, index, bibliography

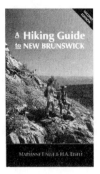

A Hiking Guide to New Brunswick, 2nd Edition

MARIANNE and H.A. EISELT

The indispensable guide to more than 90 hiking trails in New Brunswick, including maps, trail descriptions, and photographs.

0-86492-188-8 / $14.95 pb
277 pp / 4.25 x 7.25
maps, photographs, index, bibliography

Trails of Fredericton

BILL THORPE

Fredericton's network of groomed trails makes the city a paradise for the self-propelled. With historical vignettes, anecdotes, and photographs.

0-86492-235-3 / $12.95 pb
105 pp / 4.25 x 7.25
maps, index, bibliography

Biking to Blissville: A Cycling Guide to the Maritimes and the Magdalen Islands

KENT THOMPSON

A delightful and trustworthy cyclist's companion to 35 scenic rides in Maritime Canada.

0-86492-154-3 / $14.95 pb
178 pp / 6 x 9
maps, index

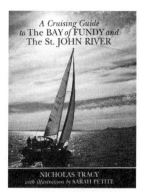

A Cruising Guide to the Bay of Fundy and the St. John River

NICHOLAS TRACY
Illustrated by SARAH PETITE

A detailed and entertaining guide to Passamaquoddy Bay, the southwestern shore of Nova Scotia, the Bay of Fundy, and the St. John River.

0-86492-129-2 / $29.95 spiral bound
200 pp / 8 x 10
illustrated, charts, index

Woodlands Canoeing: Pleasure Paddling on Woodland Waterways

RICK SPARKMAN

The fundamentals of recreational canoeing where the channels are narrow, the water is swift, and canoeing changes with the seasons.

0-86492-234-5 / $16.95 pb
155 pp / 6 x 9
illustrated

Paddling in Paradise: Sea Kayaking Adventures in Atlantic Canada

ALISON HUGHES

This charming guide describes eight enchanting coastal trips. It also tells how to find a guide, where to camp, what to pack, and how best to enjoy a foray into the wild blue ocean.

0-86492-340-6 / $19.95 pb
144 pp / 6 x 8.5
maps, photographs, index, bibliography

Bugging the Atlantic Salmon

MICHAEL BRISLAIN

A guide to the greatest of all angling experiences —
trying to outwit the wily Atlantic salmon. With
step-by-step instructions, drawings, and photos.

0-86492-161-6 / $14.95 pb
104 pp / 6 x 9
maps, illustrated (colour and b&w)

Currents in the Stream

WAYNE CURTIS

An affectionate look at people and places along the
famous Miramichi River.

0-86492-092-X / $12.95 pb
214 pp / 5.5 x 8.5
illustrated

River Guides of the Miramichi

WAYNE CURTIS

The mystique of the river rubs off on its people. Wayne
Curtis, writer and guide, introduces the river guides of
the Miramichi in a lively collection of portraits in words
and photographs.

0-86492-224-8 / $14.95 pb
186 pp / 5.5 x 8.5
illustrated, index

Safe and Sound: How Not to Get Lost in the Woods and How to Survive If You Do
GORDON SNOW

Survival tips, common sense preparations, and advice from a veteran Mountie with more than 200 rescues to his credit.

0-86492-222-1 / $9.95 pb
84 pp / 4.25 x 7
illustrated

To order these books, contact your local bookseller or:

GOOSE LANE EDITIONS
469 King Street
Fredericton, NB
Canada   E3B 1E5
Toll Free: 1 (888) 926 8377
Fax: (506) 459 4991
e-mail: gooselane@nb.aibn.com
web: http://www.gooselane.com

HIKING TRAILS OF NOVA SCOTIA

8th EDITION

Also by Michael Haynes

Hiking Trails of Cape Breton
Trails of Halifax Regional Municipality